Home by Nine

The Real Story of Portsmouth's South End

An Autobiography by

Harold Whitehouse Jr.

Harold Whitehouse Jr.

To Brenda:

4/26/08

Peter E. Randall Publisher LLC
Portsmouth, New Hampshire
2008

Peter E. Randall Publisher, LLC
Box 4726, Portsmouth, NH 03802

ISBN 1-931807-69-8

Additional copies available from the author at
58 Humphrey's Court
Portsmouth, NH 03801

Jacket front photo: Harold and granddaughter Kylie.

To my mother, Grace Berry Whitehouse
1908-2004

Preface

THE SOUTH END OF PORTSMOUTH, NEW HAMPSHIRE, is one of the most historical and oldest parts of this seacoast city. Its distinct area is separated from the rest of the city by the adjoining section known as Puddle Dock.

These are memories of my childhood of growing up in this area. It is not to say that time has drastically changed the South End, but the trials and tribulations that our large family endured during 1930–1950 are interesting.

I am very fortunate to have lived and remembered a time of prohibition, the Depression, World War II, and a recession. After the Korean War, there was Urban Renewal, historical preservation, Strawbery Banke, and economic development. Today, the South End is a Mecca for the middle class and wealthy, with many newcomers seeking a part of Portsmouth's history.

This volume is the result of three-and-a-half years of data collecting, interviewing, editing, and proofing. Some of the photos are from my collection, while others are copies of Portsmouth as it was in the bygone era.

I am indebted to Lars (a reporter) who recorded and prepared this text over a two-year period. Also to Judy and Erica of R.M.C. Research Corp., who edited and proofread the first draft of this book. Peter Randall prepared this autobiography for publication. These individuals are not responsible for any errors or shortcomings of these events.

Lastly, I thank my mother, who lived to be ninety-six years young, for giving me the genes of memory and longevity. The nine o'clock curfew, "home by nine," has long disappeared, but my mother's memories live on.

Harold Whitehouse Jr.
A True South Ender

Baby Harold Whitehouse with his mother and grandmother. (below) Hospital bill for the birth of Harold Whitehouse.

Chapter One: Beginnings
1928-1940

I WAS BORN ON JULY 1, 1928, AT PORTSMOUTH HOSPITAL, in Portsmouth, New Hampshire. My father and mother lived on Hanover Street in three rooms in a boarding house. The house has been demolished—it was near Fleet Street on Hanover. That was a big, big huge rooming house. I don't remember anything about the place. I was only four when we moved from there.

My mother's maiden name was Grace Berry. My dad's name was Harold Enoch Whitehouse. I never took his middle name. My mother was twenty when she had me and, by the time she was thirty she had six children. I was the oldest.

My mother never worked outside the home—she stayed home and took care of all us children. My father did not have a full-time job when I was young. He only had part-time work— working for the city, like mowing lawns, shoveling snow, and odd jobs. He'd get part-time jobs at the coal wharf. At the time, there were two coal wharves: Consolidated Coal Wharf and Walker Coal Wharf. He used to shovel coal out of the roadway, so the trucks could get in and load the coal as it was being offloaded from the boats. Like the salt, coal was unloaded by crane into the stockpiles— and his job would be shoveling the coal off the road.

It was day to day. The men gathered downtown and employers would come by early in the morning and pick three or four of the men who were hanging around, maybe a dozen men hanging around, at the square. This was the early '30s; there was no work. This was the Depression. My father had taken a three-month course in Boston as an automobile mechanic and still he could get no work.

When I was about age four we moved to 92 Brewster Street. The house was very small. It was the first house we ever rented with a rent of probably sixteen to seventeen dollars a month. It was down by the tracks and I remember putting pennies down on the tracks. The trains came by

1

Baby Harold Whitehouse and his father.

three or four times a day so I always had a couple of flat pennies in my pocket. We used to find Indian head pennies and, rather than spend them, I put them on the tracks. We thought that was cool. If you could show a penny that was flattened out by a train, then you were kind of king of the neighborhood.

We were the only family living in the Brewster Street house. It was a small home, in between two other larger homes. It was probably built in the early 1900s and it had a front porch, but no cellar. There was only one problem, it didn't have a cellar.

I slept upstairs in the back room. By that time my mother started having other children. I think we had three children by the time we moved from there, which was 1935. I remember collecting coal about a quarter mile up the tracks. There was a curve and, as the train came down, the coal would fall off the car. That was a real privilege—to have coal for the fire in the stove. We burned wood most of the time, but to get coal—we couldn't afford to buy it—that was great. We'd usually get our wood out in the street, along the tracks, washed up in the millpond. We lived by the millpond and there was a lot of old stuff that floated in with the tide that gathered up. We also went to the dump on Jones Avenue to collect wood.

The first one down from the upstairs would put their feet in the oven because it was so cold upstairs when we woke up. It was cold, real cold. I had a glass of water beside the bed and it always would freeze. By that time there was my brother Bobby and my sister June. Bob was born at Christmas time in 1929. My sister June was born in 1930.

The neighborhood was poor. I remember the grocery store around the corner, Mitchell's Store on Sudbury Street, I think. When my father had a job and got some money, he went around to the store to get some meat. Mitchell would always have a special package for us. Come to find out later on, it was horsemeat he was putting away for us. My mother would never tell us. It was less expensive and my mother cooked it up with some onions and it tasted wonderful. But she would never tell us, she told me later in life. Even then she was hesitant about telling us.

Across the street was the Diamond Match Lumber Company. I liked to sneak over and climb around the lumber and smell the sawdust. It was a big sawmill and there was milled lumber in its big shed. The doors were open during the summer and I used to watch them mill lumber, and that's probably how I got started on my carpentry hobby. When the yard foreman caught me climbing underneath the stacked lumber, going up and down, he chased me off the lumber pile. He was concerned about the lumber falling on me or my getting stuck and not being able to get out. The lumber was stacked four and five stories high, but I loved climbing in and out of the lumber.

We didn't go out very often. There were no other kids and I had to stay in the yard—very strict. We lived on a dead-end street. I remember the horses coming down and plowing us out, probably about four or five days after a storm. I remember, in those days, when a severe snowstorm struck, we shoveled ourselves out or waited four or five days for the horse to plow us out. I remember very distinctly the horse-drawn plows coming down the street. They put the snow off to one side; it was never taken away. In those days when we had severe storms and the snow was over the fence, we tunneled our way out.

I remember watching a parade on Fourth of July on Islington Street. It was the American Legion Parade and included a Forty-and-Eight train replica, a part of the American Legion and a symbol for the post. There was also a city band, not a school band—the biggest band in the parade, with a lot of musicians who played part-time as a hobby. People always turned out. There were a lot of flags, marching units—every organization had a marching unit, like the Masons and the Commandery, the Boy Scouts, the Rainbow Girls, and the Demolay. These latter two were the fraternal organizations of the Masons; members would go to the convales-

Neighbors shoveling snow on South School Street (above) and Pray Street.

Walter Woods often made snow sculptures to entertain the neighborhood children.

cent homes during the holidays and sing. There was also a joint dance with the boys and the girls at the Masonic Temple.

Early Christmas Memories on Brewster Street

I remember some of my toys being taken away from me and missing them, little cars and trucks. This would be around October and November and, come to find out, my father had taken them to shine them up and polish them and wrap them. The old toys would be under the tree to make sure I had something. By then, I had forgotten all about them or thought I had lost them myself. My father had a way of making them look new and under the tree they'd go. We usually went out and tried to find our tree someplace in a field and cut it down. Usually by the railroads tracks we'd find something. It might not be a Christmas tree, but a pine tree and we'd decorate it. We all had stockings, no fireplace—we hung them on the wall. If we were bad we got coal in the stocking. I got coal many, many times. We'd always get a tangerine and one little gift—a comb or a brush, anything.

I remember our next door Brewster Street neighbor cutting wood using an homemade saw operated by an old gasoline engine that was run by a belt. That was one reason why we later moved: the noise that saw made all summer long until the snow came! It kept the younger kids awake and I remember my mother getting upset because the kids would cry, cry, and cry.

The Brewster house has been repainted and it looks like a pretty nice house now. One thing I remember, and it changed my attitude about fires. I had an interest in seeing matches burn and would light a whole book of matches. I found some papers and leaves and I went underneath the porch one day and lit the matches. I think I was four or five years old. I'll never forget that. I got a little spanking. My father kept a strap behind the stove. It was there, mostly for looks, but we knew what it was for—if you did anything real bad. I got hit across the back of the legs for almost burning the porch down. If my mother hadn't come when smoke was coming up through the floor of the porch, if she hadn't gone in to get a big bucket of water, and if she hadn't thrown it in just as I was crawling out, the house might have burned down. I hid in the lumberyard and I didn't come home all day. I never touched matches again. I'm scared to death of fires.

I went to first grade at the Whipple School on State Street on the corner of Summer and State. My first day I didn't mind—but I don't even remember my teacher. I do remember taking my brother to school and I had an awful time with him. There were long stairways on the first floor and he was crying and kicking and screaming and I was in charge—my mother assigned me to take him the first day.

We didn't stay on Brewster Street for very long, only until I was seven years old. In 1935 we moved to 76 South School Street. It was a double house and we rented the front part. It was only $18 a month and the house was owned by F.A. Gray, owner of the downtown paint and hardware store, still open to this day. My father knew Mr. Gray. It was three stories and six rooms, two in the attic, two upstairs and two on the first floor—but no bath. The only toilet was in the basement. This house was right next to the Haven School.

At school we had to sit with our hands folded, all in a row. We were assigned a seat so the teacher would know where we were and so she would know all our names. There were inkwells in the desk and the top of the desks opened up. We wrote with ink from the inkwell. I could walk to school. There were no cars on the road, so it was safe. The school is now a condominium.

We had a wood-burning stove at home with registers going up to the second floor but, on the third floor where my brother and I slept, there was no heat at all. We shared a bed. You had to double up during the wintertime. My parents had the room directly up above the wood stove.

We cooked on a wood stove. I used to hate to cut the wood, but we had to do it to survive in the winter. And we would buy a bag of coal, and it was like gold. We used to take one little trowel full and put it on top of the wood. We went every Saturday morning to the dump off Jones Avenue. We had an old 1929 Essex car, and my father and I would cut wood, old scraps from construction or old lumber that people had thrown away, or that had washed up on shore someplace. Saturday was the only day the dump trucks didn't come in, so the dump was open to the public. Other people were down there dump picking, too. I found my first bike down there. I got the frame one week and two weeks later found the wheels and we put a bike together.

I loved to make model airplanes and used to hang them up in my bedroom with a piece of string. The ceilings were slanted so I could only use a portion of the room. Nothing on the walls; we weren't allowed to do that since we didn't own the house. In the living room we had the radio and the sofa and the chairs. We had a Philco dial radio; we thought that was a big deal. We pushed a button for the station we wanted—WHEB,

Whitehouse family home at 76 School Street.

WEEI or WBZ—and we turned the dial until it stopped on that station. That was state-of-the-art. I listened to everything—The Shadow, Inner Sanctum, Gangbusters, Fibber McGee and Molly, and Amos & Andy. On Sunday nights we listened to Major Bowles's Amateur Hour. My father always had certain programs he listened to late at night, but we had the radio in the afternoon. When we moved to the South End we had a hand cranked Victrola and a lot of records—mostly old swing music, big band stuff, always listened to Jimmy Dorsey, Tommy Dorsey, and Gene Krupa. I loved the drums.

My mother took me to the movies and I remember going by train to Boston when I was eight years old and we saw Louis Armstrong, old Satchmo, in person at the RKO Theatre. That was one of the biggest thrills.

Then there came Gene, Barbara, and Audrey. all living on South School Street. There were a lot of children at the end of South School Street. All large families, plenty of children to play with and we were right beside the Haven School playground, which was a place where everybody gathered. We were living in heaven. We had our own half a house with plenty of room and a playground across the street.

I asked my mother, "Were we considered poor?" And she would say, "Don't ever say that word. We're just unfortunate. We don't have the things that your friend Ralph and his mother and father have at their house." Ralph's father worked at the Shipyard and he had a supervisory job over there. He was what we called a "white hat." When I went up to Ralph's house, I was amazed to see an electric stove and a refrigerator. I couldn't believe it, all that beautiful white. We had an icebox and I was in charge of dumping the pan under it and, if it ran over, boy, I got talked to. We used to put the sign in the window to say what sized piece of ice we wanted twice a week, usually on a Monday and a Friday. Twenty-five cents, fifteen cents, ten cents for the sizes. We'd wait for the iceman to come and he'd chip off some pieces—we'd all gather around the ice truck—for us on a hot summer day.

One thing that stays in my mind is a class called "opportunity" at the Haven School, which wasn't in any of the other seven schools in Portsmouth. I found out later this was an experimental class being done for the first time. Buses would bring all the handicapped students, the slow learners, and special education children. There were about twelve or fourteen kids and they came from all over the city. And, as little children growing up in the South End, most of us boys used to stare at them as they got off the bus. They used to bus them in twice or three times a week. Each one of them had a little bit different look about them, walked a little differently, and talked differently. They were all handicapped children. They had special teachers and played with us at recess time and we stared a lot. That was, according to my mother, very embarrassing for them. My mother said, "Don't you do that." Portsmouth did the class on its own and it was the first special education program for Portsmouth. There were no grants or federal funding. It was something the city felt had to be done since these children were not getting a proper education at other schools.

Haven School.

The regular school day started at eight o'clock in the morning and we had recess about ten and went home for lunch around noontime and came back again at one. School ended at 3 or 3:30. I think my teacher's name was Miss Grant, in the second or third grade.

We stayed in the same room and one teacher taught us everything; reading, social studies, writing, and arithmetic. During recess we had a little sports program. The janitor acted as the athletic director. One of them was Reggie Dow and after he retired, Arthur Clough came in. Clough was the social studies teacher, the physical education director, the janitor, the head maintenance person, and the psychologist. He died in his nineties and they named the baseball field after him; it's Clough Field, and they named the street going into Little Harbour School Clough Drive.

We played a lot of games. It may sound funny to say now, but we played hopscotch. We enjoyed playing hopscotch—taking a rock, marking off a box on the sidewalk, and finding a piece of worn glass. We played marbles and nearsies-to-the wall with our playing cards. The cards were bought with bubble gum and identified various airplanes. We swapped cards, swapped marbles, swapped comic books, and spent hours just sit-

Haven School third grade students, ca. 1905.

ting and saying "I'll take this." We bartered, just a half dozen children in a circle. It was an enjoyable afternoon. "You want my marble?" "Okay, I want your comic book." "Give me two marbles for that comic book." I wasn't a tough negotiator, not really.

I had a big collection of comic books. I also had a big bag of marbles, which were called glassies and beauties. I don't know what ever happened to them, but I had a large collection at one time.

I was an average student. There were six of us kids, and we all helped each other in our schoolwork. Only one of us went to college, but I liked school. What was really unusual in the Haven School was the boys entered one door and the girls entered another door. We then came up a common stairway and went to our classrooms and the girls' room and the boys' room were in the basement.

"Racial" wasn't even a word to us, we wouldn't have known what it meant. The South End was an area where the rents were very cheap and families of different nationalities who were struggling moved there. The Irish and the Jewish and the Italians and the blacks were all mixed in. It wasn't like the North End where it was strictly the Italians or the Lafayette

School section where the Jewish community lived. The South End was a complete mix and we played together and worked together and swam together.

It was a place where families came to get their start—very much so. We heard different accents and it was comical because we would be taught a word a week. As we got older, an Italian or a Jewish person would teach us a word and we mingled together and it was a lot of fun. We knew better than to swear.

People did all their shopping in their local grocery store. Everybody had their own neighborhood store and we in the South End had the most. There were probably seven little grocery stores, neighborhood stores within a quarter of a mile. I can still name the stores. Downs's Store was located at the foot of South School Street, on Marcy Street. Freedman's store was up on Marcy Street, across from the Portsmouth Meeting House. Pappas's store was on the corner of Mt. Vernon Street and South Street. The South End Market was on the corner of Marcy Street and South Mill Street. Across from Mill Street, where there is a senior housing project now, there was a First National Store; it hung out over the water on pilings in an old converted building. Going up Marcy Street, just 200 or 300 feet from the corner of Marcy and Pleasant, there was an A&P. One more store was around the corner of my house, where my mother would send me up to get a penny stick of gum. My mother loved to chew gum, and they would open up a packet, and I'd bring home a stick of gum for her. She'd break it in two and give me half. That store was located on the corner of Blossom Street and South Street. It was called Weiner's and they were so good to us children.

At each store we ran a tab because my father didn't have much money and they knew we were a large family. They'd keep a tab and put it right underneath the counter. Then, when my father got work, I'd take fifty cents here or seventy-five cents and pay one bill off, and the next month pay the other bill off. My mother and my father would send me to the store with a note.

The South End was very distinct. Its boundary started at the corner of Marcy and Pleasant Streets, by the bridge, and ran down to Newcastle Avenue and up Newcastle Avenue to South Street, then up to Junkins Avenue and around the playgrounds and back down Pleasant Street. That circular area was considered the South End. Beyond the corner of Pleasant and Marcy Street heading north would be Puddle Dock. Along the waterfront, around Prescott Park, Strawbery Banke, Peirce Island Bridge, and

The heart of the South End: Newcastle Avenue to Pleasant Street, to Parrott Avenue, to Lincoln Avenue to Miller Avenue to South Street and along the back channel.

Bow Street—that was all Puddle Dock. Then there was Christian Shore, the creek, and the Lafayette School District, which was where most of the merchants and businesspeople lived. There were beautiful homes all along Lafayette Road, Middle Street, and the western end of South Street.

The Hurricane of 1938

It was a September day and it rained all night and we went to school the next day. For some reason, we didn't know why, they let us go home early. At home my mother said, "I want all of you children to get into the house now." It started getting dark and it was very scary because it was in the afternoon, three or four o'clock. It was pitch dark. And then the wind came up, worse, and by six o'clock it was really howling and my mother sent us all to bed. We went up to our rooms and pulled the curtains and the wind was howling. I was ten years old and my brother was nine. We lost a big tree out front and all the power lines went down. It was scary and my brother and I talked about it for years afterwards. We swore the bed moved.

The rain came right through the windows and sounded like a locomotive. The windows were so old and shattered that the rains drove right through. All the blankets on one side of the bed were soaked. My brother and I unplugged the radio—that was all we had that was electrical. We were under the covers. No one knew what was happening. We knew we were going to get a storm, but no one foresaw that it was going to be a hurricane.

The next morning we got up and couldn't believe the damage. Most of the trees, the wires, and the telephone poles were down. The houses in the South End were built fairly rugged. The storm took a fence here and there—a tree would go down across the fence or across some wires. There was a lot of debris all over the place; along the waterfront and all over the roads. It was weeks before it was cleaned up. Usually if a road was impassable in your section and you were on a side road you took care of it yourself. There was no school the next day and I remember the adults didn't allow us to venture too far away. We couldn't go down to where the store was on Marcy Street or anywhere near Marcy Street or the waterfront. The men came around in the trucks days afterwards. They cut everything up by hand—no chain saws then—and took it away in the truck. We kept a portion of the big old oak tree that came down in front of my house.

Shipyard

By this time—around 1938—my father had a part-time job at the Navy Yard as a laborer. He worked in public works, mostly at odd jobs cutting lawns and shrubbery mostly up near the officers' quarters. There were a lot of beautiful homes on the Shipyard where the officers and their families lived. My father was proud to be working at the Portsmouth Naval Shipyard even though it was only three to four hours a day.

We were a very close family. It was important that we ate together at five o'clock every night. My mother prepared the best meal she could for the evening meal but I didn't like corn chowder, even today I don't because I had so much of it. I would go down to the creamery for my mother and get a jug of skim milk for nine cents and then get a can of corn for ten cents. We had corn chowder for breakfast, at noontime, and in the evening. She also made corn fritters and corn bread; everybody grew corn in their gardens, too. I've had enough of it.

Marget Square, circa 1935. My father and other men would wait at the corner of Congress and High Streets hoping someone would come by needing workers.

The creamery was located on Bow Street, which was just around the corner from the Memorial Bridge, where Harbor Place is. It's now the St. John's Church parking lot. That was Badger's Farm Creamery. If you took a gallon jug, you could have a whole gallon of skim milk for nine cents. It was a little bit of a walk, but my mother allowed me to do that.

We didn't venture very far downtown, but we took lots of walks every Sunday. My father loved to walk. Here I was, ten, eleven years old, and we'd take a Sunday walk to the potato chip factory on Sagamore Avenue just beyond Sagamore Bridge. That was Ladd's Potato Chip Factory on Sagamore Avenue. We took a paper bag with us and got broken chips, free; they wouldn't charge us at all and that was a big deal. We'd bring them home and we'd each have a small portion and we'd put the chips in another little bag. That was our treat. Then we'd sit around listening to the radio on Sunday night and we'd all have our little bag of chips. My mother made Kool-Aid and that was a nice little get-together. Even now, a portion of the Seacoast Mental Health building can be identified as Ladd's Potato Chip Factory.

There was not a lot to do in Portsmouth. There were no jobs here, and we saw how our families struggled and we didn't like it. Many of us

Downes Store.

left and many of us tried to get back and couldn't get back. It was too expensive.

In my neighborhood there were some storeowners I'll never forget. Downs's Store, with an old gas pump outside, was probably the first lobster pound in the city, at the end of South School Street on Marcy Street. Downs was a huge man, with hands like baseball mitts. A fisherman, he was probably six-foot-six and I'd see him come in carrying a crate of lobsters. He probably weighed 250-275 pounds and he always treated us kids wonderfully. He had a pinball machine in the back room—the first store

One of the first lobster pounds, corner of Marcy and South School streets.

that ever had a pinball machine. We found a way to undo some screws on the glass, slide the glass down and then knock off about a dozen games. We'd stay there for hours on a cold day or a stormy day and he knew what we were doing. But he loved having kids in the store. In the back room he knew where we were and we weren't getting into any trouble. We needed one nickel to start the game.

During the summer, as the people traveled back and forth to the Wentworth by the Sea Hotel in New Castle—a posh resort—we'd be amazed at the chauffeurs and the big Cadillacs and the Lincolns that would pull up. And the chauffeur would open the door for a little old lady draped in furs or a gentleman dressed in a three-piece suit and top hat, and they'd buy some lobsters and be taken to the Wentworth. We'd stand there and see those big, huge, monstrous cars and we'd look and look, so shiny. We'd never seen anything like that before.

Survival

In order to survive we had to plan for each season. We planned for the winter and then we made preparations for a spring garden. Everybody had a garden. If you had a plot as big as a kitchen table in your back yard, you had a garden. Many families had chickens—we didn't—but the people in back of us had a dozen and they had eggs all the time. In WWII we had a Victory Garden. The landowners divided all the land off Pleasant Point off Newcastle Avenue, which is now a housing subdivision, but back then it was all open, with beautiful soil. We had a plot down there during the war where we grew vegetables. Vegetables were the backbone of surviving during the wintertime. We canned tomatoes and string beans and corn. Every night—I can hear my father now—"Junior get the rake and the hoe in the car—we're going to the garden." The old 1929 Essex had a trunk and I had to put the tools in the trunk.

In 1939 there was the sinking of the *Squalus*. We had heard about it and we knew the *Herald* was going to put out an Extra but we had already started on our paper route. Every person who had a paper route at the *Portsmouth Herald* had a helper and I was the helper. Our route was up on South Street, so we ran back to where the papers were being printed at the old *Herald* office at 82 Congress Street and waited for the Extra to come out because that was news. They put out the Extra and we sold it on the street. I bought probably ten papers. You bought the papers for three cents, as many as you wanted, and sold it for five cents. We didn't have any trouble selling them, especially around the "beer joints" downtown.

The sinking was a terrible thing. We got into the car, the whole family did, and we went down to Wallis Sands Beach and we could see the ships maneuvering off the Isles of Shoals. We couldn't see too much because it was way off shore, but we had a heavy-duty set of spyglasses that we kids looked through and we could see the rescue boats out there and the Momson Bell. We went down there two or three nights in a row. We didn't see the sub surface; never saw that famous buoyancy of the bow as it came out of the water. But when it was being towed into Portsmouth we did go to Peirce Island and see it brought back.

How 33 in Sea Tomb Met Fate

From white-lipped heroes whose haggard faces and haunted eyes still showed the strain of an ordeal of prolonged horror, came yesterday the graphic stories of just what happened after the Squalus sank to the floor of the sea and became a prison for the living and a tomb for the dead.

Items from Harold's **Squalus** *scrapbook. Top image shows the bow of the sub at the first attempt to raise her from the sea bottom. The bow appeared for a few moments then sank again, but was successfully raised later.*

At that time my mother made me keep a scrapbook, and I still have it today, from all that happened and how the *Squalus* was raised . I go through it on the anniversary each May. Gerald "Mac" McLees of Portsmouth, one of the thirty-three men rescued by the Momson Bell, died recently at the age of 90. I attended his funeral.

It was very important we went to church—the Christ Episcopal Church. We would go every single Sunday. We all had to line up to make sure our shoes were shined. The pastor was Father Walker. That church burned and that's where the apartments are on Madison Street today. It was a huge stone church and it should have been salvaged. It burnt and all the stone was left intact, but the whole innards and the old creosote-type timbers and all the flooring just disintegrated.

In Sunday school we would hear stories of the times, whatever period it was during the year. It could be a story of Christmas, the crucifixion story on Good Friday, the story of Easter; or the story of Passover. Father Walker would sit on the edge of the pew and we'd be facing him and he'd tell a different story. He had two classes, one for the very young, from about six to ten and then another for ten to about fifteen, sixteen.

The South End

It was a very poor neighborhood. In fact, when we ventured into another neighborhood people could tell where we were from. They could either smell fish on us or look at our clothes. We were made fun of in a sense. Many times I was invited to the North End because I had a cousin who lived in the North End, on Deer Street, which was the Italian section. After he introduced me to all his friends I was accepted. My mother would take me up there to her sister's and they'd sit and talk and have lunch all day and I'd be out and around the neighborhood with my cousin who was the same age as I was. But I was accepted because he introduced me to them at a young age.

No one came down to the South End unless they came to play basketball. We had the only hot-topped striped court in the city, an official regulation basketball court at the Haven School playground. All year long, even during the winter, we'd shovel in the morning and have a game with another section of the city in the afternoon, on a Saturday or a Sunday.

Our playground equipment was unique. We had a seesaw and monkey bars, which we thought were out of the ordinary. Not too many

The circus comes to Brackett Field.

schools had monkey bars. While the basketball court was hot-topped, the rest of the playground was all gravel.

At about eleven years old, I remember my father telling me that if I did all my chores around the house he would take me somewhere special early one morning. So he woke me up about three o'clock, and said, "Get dressed, Junior, you're going to see the circus." I couldn't understand what he meant. So we walked downtown to the railway station on Deer Street and we saw a circus come in by train. We saw the elephants unload, the tigers in a cage being put on a truck, and the clowns all dressed up. There were a few kids, but not too many. They probably didn't want to get up that early. We saw the circus parade go through town at six o'clock in the morning. It went right straight through Congress Street, right up Junkins Avenue to Brackett Field. Brackett Field was right off South Street where the Little Harbour School is now. It was a wide-open field and that's where the circus tents were set up. It was one of the biggest thrills of my life, seeing the circus train come in and unload down at the railroad station and follow the circus parade through town. My mother and father always found money to take us to the circus.

Later, the circuses came by truck, and we had a circus every summer down at Brackett Field and, as I got older, I worked the circus. In exchange for a free ticket, I'd help carry the timbers that were used for the bleacher seats and I'd get hay and water for the elephants. In those days you determined how big a circus was by the number of elephants it had and they always had a half a dozen and huge tents. It took from six o'clock in the morning to one o'clock in the afternoon to get the circus ready and then it went on at two. They had a seven o'clock performance in the evening and then they were gone. I couldn't believe it. I'd go down to the field because it was a short distance from my house and they'd be gone. Everything packed up. You wouldn't even recognize a circus had been in that place.

There were other attractions that came through town. Over on Badger's Island in Kittery there was a carnival but I was never allowed to go over there because it was quite a ways across Memorial Bridge.

During the summer we went swimming at the end of Ridges Court, which is a street off Newcastle Avenue. All the families would gather and take their children and their chairs and old camping stools. At high tide you had two or three hours of beautiful swimming because the water would be warm. It backed up into a channel and it was very safe. We walked out very gradually and one hundred yards off shore we'd only be up to our waist.

The mothers would sit there and knit and tell stories and it would be like a neighborhood gathering. We did that many a summer afternoon.

Directly across from the school grounds a family of four moved in with a boy my age. His name was Bob and we became friendly. We saw in a *Popular Mechanics* magazine that you could take a can and put a hole in the bottom and run a string from one can to the other and if it was waxed, you could use the contraption as a telephone. So we decided to buy some string—we found it for ten cents a roll up around the corner at South End Market—and we perfected our "telephone." We waxed the string and strung it across the Haven School playground from his bedroom to my bedroom. We had probably 150 feet of string running across the playground and if you pulled the string tight you could hear yourself talk. We thought that was pretty neat—until some wise little kid saw the string going from one house to the other and threw a rock with a piece of string tied to it and pulled our string down along with both screens out of my window and his. My father stopped that project right away.

During the summer we'd stay out until the streetlights were on—once they were on you had to be home. And the city had a nine o'clock curfew. When you heard the nine o'clock alarm go off, most kids under sixteen had to be in the house. The police didn't come down, not too often. Not in the South End. It wasn't unsafe. There weren't any fancy cars or fancy clothes or fancy furniture or any fancy houses. But families watched out for each other, it was a close-knit section of the city to live in.

I stayed at the Haven School from 1935 until 1940, when I was twelve years old. My life was beginning to change a little bit. I was able to ride my bike out of the neighborhood. I was entering the junior high. That building, I thought, was gorgeous. It had only been built about thirteen years before. I entered the building with its huge pillars and marble floor, all polished. The ceiling looked like the heavens. It had clouds and indirect lighting and stars and, if you looked closely, you could see the clouds almost moving.

So, going into that school with books in hand and my friends beside me heading to our assigned room was really a change for me. There I was, away from my home. I was finally venturing a little way outside my neighborhood, which wasn't allowed until I got to be twelve years old.

Harold, seated second from left, and his brother Bobby, right, at the Christmas party for the morning route paperboys. They worked for news dealer Harry Winebaum, top right. (below) Harold in his Boy scout uniform, and his Herald *newspaper boy badge.*

Chapter Two: Growing Up

At the beginning of World War II, there was a little more work and people were beginning to update some of the houses. A few of the landlords were redoing the porches and allowing tenants to paint inside or wallpaper. They'd allow us, if we had a little carpentry experience, to put in new steps going up to the second or third floor, or put a railing in, or repair the back steps leading out of the house. Things like that. The landlords would buy the materials and we'd do the work.

My father and I did an awful lot of work on the front section of the house. My father was still a part-time worker at the Shipyard. Our economic situation was getting a little bit better. That's when I bought a paper route for $2, delivering the *Portsmouth Herald* on my bike. We picked up our papers at the back of the old *Herald* office, which was on Porter Street and I'd walk all the way up Middle Road to the Lafayette School area. It was Route 22, which was a nice section of the city. It started at the old Lafayette School District, which was kind of the wealthiest part of the city, and extended all the way down to the corner of Newcastle Avenue and South Street—all those houses, all the side streets. I had 120 papers to deliver. During real severe snowstorms I wouldn't use my bike. I'd walk.

Those people took very good care of me at Christmas time. They tipped heavily. They knew I came from a large family. They knew my mother and father. My mother would make a batch of fudge and I would sell pieces of fudge all wrapped in wax paper for five cents each from a box. I'd have the whole box sold—maybe thirty-five or forty pieces—bought by the people from along South Street. By the time I got to Miller Avenue it was gone. My mother loved to bake and her fudge was unbelievable. I got so many compliments about that. I'd pay my mother for the ingredients and the following week or so when she got some spare time she would make me another batch and I'd do the same thing. Many times during the summer this gave me a little extra money.

I'll never forget the time I bought a suit from Sears Roebuck. It cost

$7 and I gave the pants to my brother who was one year younger but the same size I was and I wore the jacket. It was my first suit jacket and I wore that quite a bit to church and to special gatherings we had at the junior high in the auditorium.

There was a time when we were getting a lot of colds, so my mother lined us all up and told us that every fall of the year we were going to have to take cod liver oil. Each one of us would take a dose of cod liver oil in the morning—we all hated it. I hated it so much I'd hold it in my mouth and gag before I'd swallow it. But I started thinking, as years went on, that if I was the one with the cold, that same spoon was being used over and over all the way down the line. I don't know what my mother was thinking. We also took Father John's medicine halfway through the winter to keep us healthy. But we ate good and had fresh vegetables a lot and we just kept warm and played outdoors a lot. That was pretty important to my mother. We'd bundle up and go outdoors and play and not come in until we were told to. My mother would always say, "The fresh air is good for you." We made our own enjoyment.

This was an exciting time for me. One of my favorite things was sitting in that auditorium at the junior high. There were huge murals on the walls that fascinated me, replicas of what Portsmouth was like in the early days. It showed the early landings on Strawbery Banke; what it was like probably to land by boat, by rowboat, coming in from the Shoals. It showed bartering with the Indians who were located inland a little ways. It showed the clipper ships coming up through the channel. They were hand-painted murals from the ceiling to the floors—huge. Several years ago, when they renovated the junior high, they ripped out the auditorium to make fourteen new classrooms. It probably was the biggest loss the city has ever had in its school system.

There was only the seventh, eighth, and ninth grade in the junior high. There wasn't room in the high school downtown for the freshman class. I don't remember my teachers except my vocational teacher. I took woodworking and printing. Mr. Volkman taught us printing. He had an old platinum press with a flywheel and a foot treadle, and that was probably my most important subject of all. I looked forward to setting type from a case, locking it up in the chase, and running a job off on the press. It wasn't motorized; you got the foot treadle to get your flywheel going to start the platinum back and forth. A roller would pick up ink from the ink drum and go over the face of the type with it.

Harold bought this old press when Randall Press moved out of its Daniel Street office in the 1960s. Identical to the one he used at the junior high, it is a Proudy #1, foot-treddled, 8.5 x 11 press.

Our school day started at about quarter to eight. Some kids took their bikes but most of the time we walked. We took a shortcut near South Street. We would walk by the Mill Pond along the wall and cut across where the playgrounds are now—we could be at the junior high in minutes.

Donald, Ralphie, and Hermy were my best friends and we played together all the time, plus my brother Bobby. We played near the South Mill Pond in an area we called "The Cliff." We even made a raft over there, Donald and I, from two 50-gallon oil drums that we found at the dump. We cut logs over at the Cliff. It was a heavy tree-growth area along the Mill Pond. There were very few houses on those side streets going down to the pond. Donald and I used the raft to go back and forth to school. There was a bridge underneath Junkins Avenue and we could pole our way under-neath the bridge over to the front of the school and tie the raft up to some weeds, and we'd also go home by raft. It was an adventure; it was excit-ing—until some kids started to throw rocks at us to keep us off shore until the bell rang. By the time we'd pole in, we'd be soaking wet. We thought they were jealous of us using the raft. These were kids from the North End. Sometimes we'd sit in the classroom with wet pants and shoes.

In the junior high we'd go from room to room for different classes: arithmetic in one room, sciences in another room, and English in another. We'd have a different teacher for each subject, but one homeroom teacher. We'd gather every morning in homeroom and when the bell rang we were assigned by schedule to the next class. We'd carry our books with us. We said the Pledge of Allegiance in the morning and even in those days one kid would read from the Bible, a little section was his choice.

Unlike the Haven School, the junior high had a real athletic director, and there was a schedule and organized intramural sports. There was no dress code; we had never even heard of a dress code. We dressed casually, nice sweaters. Most of the time you had a necktie on and a pair of pants. At first we wore knickers and then those went out of style and, after I was made fun of a couple of times, my mother was able to get me a pair of long pants.

I wasn't very studious. I took the simplest courses just to get by. I liked the mechanical courses, all the vocational courses. I took woodworking and still have an item I made in the seventh grade, a little cutting board shaped like a pig. I brought that home as a Christmas gift for my mother.

We did not hear much about what was going on in the outside world. There were headlines in the paper about what was happening in Europe and Poland and Austria, but we weren't paying too much attention to it. It was not even mentioned in the schools.

After school was over, we went to the Jones Avenue dump to collect junk. Copper, aluminum, and rags were worth money. I became friendly with a kid named Jack in the seventh grade who lived on Washington Street. He took me down and introduced me to the junk dealers off Washington Street in the Puddle Dock area: Sam Hooz, Zeidman, and Sam Hooz, Jr. They would buy aluminum, and rags. Once we found that out, we went to the dump many afternoons in the summer and after school, even up to when the snow flew. I can see myself now coming down South Street on my bike with a long copper pipe tied to my basket on the front of my bike. We'd have to get it home because the junk dealers wouldn't take it if it was any longer than a foot, so I'd have to get my father's hacksaw. We spent hours out in the back yard cutting copper into foot-long pieces so we could put it in a box and take it down. Since the junk dealer paid by weight, we would spend hours crushing old aluminum pot or pan with two stones, trying to compact it because we thought it added weight to it. We really believed the more we compacted it the heavier it got. As I got older, of course, I realized it didn't change the weight whatsoever.

We'd even spend hours in the backyard with a jackknife, stripping insulation off wire to get to the copper. We'd roll it up into a ball to get some money. Back then a burlap bag of rags was worth seventy-five cents. We tried putting some window weights in the middle of the bag, but that didn't fool the dealers. They knew what a bag of rags would weigh and they'd give us just what was called for, nothing more and nothing less. I don't

Harold and his friends sold junk to dealer Sam Hooz at the corner of Hancock and Washington streets, today's Strawbery Banke Museum.

know what they used the rags for but, to us, a bag of rags was worth gold.

We knew that money would get us to the movies, would buy us things. There just wasn't any money coming from the family and there wasn't any such thing as an allowance. In fact, when I was 13 years old, my mother found out that I was doing so well on my paper route that I had to pay board! But she fooled me because she put the money in a little bank account. She didn't tell me, but when I got a little older, in high school, she gave me the bankbook.

My parents were strict, very strict. There were times when I had to be in and couldn't do the other things the kids were doing I thought they were being a little mean to me. But it was just concern—they didn't want anything happening to me.

There was the time my mother found out I rode my bike downtown and rode below Peavey's Hardware Store on Market Street. That was a no-no; you never ventured below Peavey's on Market Street. That was the tough section, the winos and hobos hung out there. It was a bad element. She found out that I rode my bike a little ways down there and my bike was taken away from me for two weeks.

South End Winters

It seemed as though the winter set in early during those years. We skated on the South Mill Pond. It wasn't unusual for the upper Mill Pond to freeze right after Thanksgiving. It was safe enough to skate on the first or second week in December. We skated all winter long because the water would never go out completely at low tide. There was a different type of dam at the lower part of the Mill Pond, down by the South End Market. It kept the water in at all times.

The ponds would freeze and there would be beautiful, beautiful skating. There would be a snowstorm the night before and by noontime half the pond would be cleared because there would be so many people down there with shovels and scrapers pushing the snow to one side.

On a beautiful Saturday night there would be bonfires on one side of the pond by the tennis courts and on the other side, where the courthouse is now, there'd be another bonfire. We'd gather wood along the shore and there'd be enough light to see everybody skating. It was a nice gathering, it really was. They had an old, old summerhouse, built like a warehouse, which was right at the end of Kent Street and that's where we gathered to put on our skates or to get a little warm. There was an old woodstove in there. If the weather were decent you'd find half the city down there. If a person came with a car radio they'd open all the doors and play the radio loud. Radios in cars were separate items back then. You had to buy the radio and rig it up yourself. A car seldom came with a radio.

Not everybody in my family skated. My father did, but my mother didn't. I told you that my father had gone to mechanic's school. As I got older he wanted to teach me a bit of what he knew. Just to keep his hands into the mechanics field he would rip out the motor of our old 1929 Essex and hang it from a tree one week and we'd put it back the next week. He wanted me to work with him and he'd try to teach me. He'd say, "Junior, hand me that watchamacallit," referring to specific tool. But even today I won't even change the oil on my own car. I despise working on an automobile engine. I had to do it on many, many a Saturday morning when the kids were playing basketball or football or enjoying themselves down swimming. I had to spend some time with my father because he thought he was doing me a big favor by teaching me what he knew.

The Whitehouse family at Dolly Copp Campground.

I was able to remove a flat tire and take a tube out of the rim, patch it and put it back again, all at the age of twelve. So, he did teach me that. It did come in handy when I had to change a flat on my bicycle. I knew exactly what to do.

Once a year we'd go camping—we'd get in the old car and go to Dolly Corp Campground, in Gorham, in the White Mountains. We'd go every year with an old tent and we'd take the whole family. My father loved to climb mountains and, by the age of twelve, I climbed Mt. Washington. At the time I was one of the youngest to get to the summit of Mt. Washington, according to the attendant at the top.

1941

That summer was routine—collecting junk, playing around the schoolyard and the Cliff. My friend Ralphie was a great reader of *Popular Science* and *Popular Mechanics*. He saw a set of plans on how to make a deep-sea diving helmet. We were able to get a five-gallon oil can and we cut a hole in it and put in a piece of glass, insulated around the glass so it wouldn't leak, got some trash-can handles and bolted them on the side of the five-gallon oil can. Then we bought thirty feet of hose, or we found thirty feet of hose, and we had a bicycle pump! We devised a system where we pumped air into the top of the helmet and then we had a valve that would take the air out through another hose. We worked on that all summer.

And, just before we entered eighth grade, we thought we'd try it. So we found a boat and went out in the middle of the Piscataqua River, right off the Portsmouth Naval Shipyard Prison. We had to make sure we got down deep. And then we said, first of all, we need to stay on the bottom. So we got some window weights and then we tied four window weights around our waists. It took us a little while to decide which one of us was going to do the pumping in the boat and which one was going down. I was the one who lost and went underwater the first time.

The helmet really worked, but I was scared. I pulled the helmet down and it kept in the air. I stayed down there on the bottom for maybe two minutes walking around and I pulled on the line and he pulled me back up. The line was around my waist. We were probably in fifteen feet of water. As long as we kept pumping, the air pressure stayed up and it would go out the top of the tube. If it hadn't worked I could've undone the knot—it was a slipknot—and the weights would have fallen to the bottom. Ralphie also went down after a while.

We also made a kayak and it didn't leak. We cut the ribs by hand, and then we covered it with canvas and melted paraffin wax. I can see us now, out in the back shed at this old gas stove melting paraffin wax. We had a big bucketful and before it cooled off we took a rag and swabbed the whole canvas kayak with this paraffin. We used quite a bit on that two-man kayak. We used it in the Little Harbour back channel area.

We also used to go trash picking. When the garbage was put out, we'd go up and down our street just taking a look to see what people had discarded. One day we found a .22 revolver. We were only thirteen years old at that time and Ralphie went home and found a .22 caliber single bullet. We went down to Brackett Field and we were holding the revolver up and we were going to fire it. Ralphie knew a little bit about guns, but I didn't. I knew nothing. I said, "I'm scared, I don't dare to do this." But Ralphie said, "Go ahead, we only have one bullet, fire it. Fire it down there, there's nobody down there, there's no houses down in that area." I said, "No, no, let's go in and put it in a vice and turn the vice around and open the window in a back shed and have the muzzle pointing out the window to an open field. We'll tie a piece of string around it and point it out the window because I'm afraid of that gun." We put it in the vice and put a string around the trigger and we pulled it and, sure enough, it blew the muzzle all to pieces. The muzzle was blocked and we hadn't even inspected it. The gun would have blown our hands right off. That was very close. We had-

Portsmouth Bicycle Park operated from 1897 until 1908 off Newcastle Avenue. By the 1930s, Harold remembers only part of the bleachers remained.

The Whitehouse children, April 1941: clockwise from top left, Robert, 11, June, 10, Gene, 5, Barbara, 2, and Harold, 12, holding Audrey, 1.

n't even looked in the barrel and that was why it was in the garbage.

We didn't have a bathroom in our South School Street house. We only had a toilet in the basement. Every Sunday night—Sunday, not Saturday—we brought the big white tub up from down cellar. It was a heavy, freestanding, white porcelain tub and I would put the papers down on the floor and we'd shut the door. We had to heat two buckets of water on the stove. This was done in the kitchen and we'd pull the shades down right beside the stove. I'd take my bath and my next duty was to dump the water out of the tub and put two new buckets of water on the stove for the next person. So when you finished your bath that water was all heated and ready to go. And it'd go from six o'clock at night until the last person, who was probably the baby. My mother would take care of her. All six of us would line up for a Sunday night bath in that tub. Then we'd take the tub back down cellar. This happened until the age of seventeen, when I went into the Navy.

In 1940, during my last year in Portsmouth Junior High, the last sister in the family, Audrey, was born. We had a nice family of six children, three boys and three girls, and father and mother made a family of eight. In those days it wasn't unusual to have large families. Everybody was born in the hospital. I said to my mother, 'Gee, you went from 1935 to 1939 without any children? What happened?' She used to laugh, "Never mind, Junior, I'll tell you later." There were six children in a matter of eleven years. I had a lot of responsibility. In fact, at the age of twelve I had two little sisters I had to take for a walk in the carriage in front of the house. Out in the schoolyard, the kids would mock me, "There goes Junior taking care of baby sister! There's Junior taking care of baby sister." But I didn't mind. I loved little children.

My dad now was working full-time at the Navy Yard. In 1939 he had received full-time status and he was very proud of that, but he was still a laborer, doing odd jobs, mowing lawns, cutting hedges, and on shift work and snow removal for public works.

Our situation was a little bit better. In fact, in 1940, we got rid of the old 1929 Essex and he bought a 1937 Dodge—still three-year old car—but it had the curtains in the window and the visor in the front. It was a big car, and on a Sunday, all eight of us got in and took a ride out to the countryside or to Stratham. My father loved to take the dirt roads of Stratham thinking he could get lost, but he never did.

Junior high was kind of exciting. It was going from room to room for different classes and some of our teachers I can remember very plain-ly. There was Raymond I. Beal, the principal of the school, who was very strict. There was Mr. Rose, Mr. Hackstrom, and Mr. Phelps, my shop teacher. I admired him very much. That was my favorite subject, wood-working. Mr. Phelps was a very nice guy and very good with the children. He had probably twenty-five or twenty-eight children in the shop class and he knew exactly what each one was doing. He preached on the safe use of hand tools. There we were, twelve years old, using the block plane, hand chisels, and the drill press—we weren't allowed to use the power saw. He taught us the safety issues, which were very important. He was an older man, had a lot of experience in carpentry, and at a later age, he had come to the school as a vocational teacher in the woodshop.

Mr. Beal was a very strict principal. In those days if you acted up—pushing in the stairwell; running in the hallway; or fighting—you were sent to the office with a note. Mr. Beal would read the note and set you out-side the office on a large deacon's bench—it was very humiliating. I remember sitting there for about a half hour and every teacher and every one of my friends went by and shook their fingers and shook their heads. That was part of the discipline, being humiliated sitting in front of the principal's office and everybody knew why you were down there.

For more serious issues, like someone fighting or talking back to a teacher, swearing at a teacher, or tripping, you had to hold out your hand and you got hit across the knuckles with a thick ruler—just one time. If you flinched, you got it twice and the first thing the kids wanted to see when you got back to the classroom was how red your knuckles were. It never happened to me but it did quite often to some friends of mine. But the biggest punishment was getting a note sent home to your mother and your mother saying, "Wait 'til your father gets home." That was when you stood up and took notice because you were in for some real trouble. In the aver-age family, when father got home, you got disciplined and never forgot it.

We made fun of Mr. Beal behind his back, a little bit. We called him Shorty Beal. He was a little guy, but he was very respected, too. When he entered the hallway, you went down the right hand side of the hallway and back on the left. You never cut across when you were going from class to class and you traveled in a row of two.

Mr. Rose, Billy Rose, was my favorite teacher besides Mr. Phelps. He taught English. I had difficulty in English starting from an early age. In fact, in my high school years, I'll tell you later on, I had to take two English classes in my senior year to get my diploma. Junior high I found very difficult. I had to do a lot of studying. No matter where I was out playing I had to come in at 7:30 and I sit over in the corner of the kitchen with a light and my book and that's where I had to study until at least nine o'clock. There was no listening to the radio during the week. The only time we could listen to the radio was Saturday and Sunday night.

We took a short cut to school. We never traveled along the road. We were able to cut in back of people's yards, across the back of the old hospital grounds, across by the playgrounds and around the Mill Pond to where the school was on Parrott Avenue. So we only crossed one street. The kids who lived in the South End loved that; everybody took that same route.

Halloween in 1940 was a time when we all traveled together as a group, four or five kids together and we did a lot of crazy things. I used to make a mask out of a paper bag, cut holes for the eyes and the mouth and then take crayons and paint the face like that of the Lone Ranger, or Tonto or cowboys like Tom Mix or Buck Jones, Then we'd go around the neighborhood and do a lot of vicious things. We'd always soap the windows of all the houses up and down the street. We'd sometimes write our initials. And then, if there was one person who had given us a bad time, like kicking us out of their backyard because we were raiding their apple tree, we'd say, "Now's the time to get even with him." We'd collect chicken manure and put it in a paper bag. Everybody had chickens in their backyards and we knew who had the most chickens and who had the most manure. We'd put chicken manure in a paper bag and then we'd try to find some horse manure some place. There were always wagons going by and on the edge of the road you could find some ripe horse manure, and then you'd stuff that in the bag also. Then we'd go to the house where this older man had given us a bad time for cutting through his property, or for watching between his curtains to make sure us kids didn't do any vandalism around his house. He just didn't like children. So we put the bag on the sidewalk in front of his house and light the bag with a match. When it was burning we'd ring his doorbell and naturally he'd come to the door and see a burning bag. He'd come down the steps and stamp out the fire and the chicken manure and the horse manure would go up through his slippers and his toes he would be furious. We'd be hiding behind the bushes laughing like anything. We did that every single Halloween. That was the biggest thing. It went on for years and years until we couldn't find any more chicken manure or horse manure and that was it.

We'd also make a rattler. We'd notch out the edge of a wooden spoon, and then wrap string around it. We'd put a pencil through a hole in the spoon like a top. We'd spin that against the window and watch the person inside who is usually listening to the radio and he'd go right through the ceiling. It makes a terrible noise on glass—inside more than outside and we'd do that time and time again. Another trick was to take a potato and stuff it in the exhaust pipe of a car parked out in front of a house, The cars had a straight pipe for the exhaust. Then when they started up in the morning, boom, and the potato would shoot down the street, like a backfire. They'd get out of the car and say, "I can't figure out what happened." The hood would go up and they'd look around underneath the car. The potato would be way down the street. So those are some of the things we did on Halloween. There really was more trick than treating.

The night before Halloween was called Beggar's Night. That's when you went out with your paper bag and went begging from house to house. They had Navy Yard Beggar's Night and regular Beggar's Night. Most of the children of the workers on the Shipyard would go out and they would be given apples and cornballs. Everybody made cornballs and wrapped them in wax paper. Everybody had candy or fudge they made at home, nobody bought anything, and you'd be given wrapped up pieces of fudge, or apples, or a tangerine. That was Beggar's Night.

Halloween was just mischievous-type movements by the kids. There was no knocking on doors saying trick or treat; I don't remember ever doing that. You made your own jack o' lanterns. You carved out a pumpkin and tied a piece of string through it and put a candle in, and then you walked down the street with a candle lit in the pumpkin. When the wind blew the candle out, everybody would look around and ask if you had any matches.

In 1940 my father allowed me to join the Boy Scouts. I joined the North Church troop 194 and stayed with the Boy Scouts for four years. The scoutmaster was Lawrence Hamilton. My father took me to his house up on Austin Street one Sunday afternoon. He called me in and interviewed me and had me fill out a form. He said, "I'll get back to you and let you know if your son can come into my troop or not." He was very proud of his troop of 30 or 35 boys.

Mr. Hamilton contacted my family and allowed me to join the troop. He said he was going to look into my academics and my school to find out if I had any discipline problems, if I was a good student. That's how he left the issue with my father. Then he contacted us and said, "We'll allow your son to be a member of our troop." I felt very proud, very proud.

Our meeting time was once a week in the afternoon in a building behind the Elk's Home at the corner of Pleasant and Court. There was a brick building in behind the Elk's. I think that building was used for carriages and horses at one time, as there were huge stalls there. That building has since been torn down.

I obtained all my twenty-one merit badges, which I still have on a sash, and I became an Eagle Scout at the age of 16. Every other Saturday, twice a month, we'd meet at headquarters and we would go on a hike. We'd have our knapsacks with us and we'd take a couple hotdogs, or a hamburger, and rolls. We'd walk out Rockingham Avenue, a wooded area, toward the old Portsmouth airport. We went across Woodbury Avenue and then we were in a complete wilderness. It would be a little over a mile out to the airport. But along the way we'd stop and build a warm little fire and cook our meal right there. We'd cook our hamburgers or hot dogs in a fry pan, which my mother had put a little bit of grease in, and some kind of potatoes that were boiled. And we had hotdogs and fried potatoes cooked out in the open.

Then we'd continue along our way and, if it was in the summer, we'd swim in Peverly Hill Brook, which is still out at Pease. It was a nice swimming hole, and then we'd hike back about two miles. Two miles out and two miles back and it was a nice Saturday afternoon.

One thing I remember was going to a scout jamboree down at Hampton Beach State Park. There were Scouts from all over New England, probably 500 or 600 camping out for a whole week on platforms. We pitched our own tent and cooked own meals and in the morning were in competition in certain games. We went to the beach in the afternoon and every day was scheduled.

I remember Andy and I were working on our cooking merit badge. Our job was to cook dinner Saturday night, franks and beans, for at least twenty-five or thirty Boy Scouts in our troop. Well, we had hot dogs on ice in a metal box in the ground. We were thinking that ice would preserve the hot dogs for a whole week. But in the middle of July ice didn't last long. We should have known better. When it came time to cook the hotdogs—I think we had ten pounds of hotdogs—they were all green and slimy. Well, we didn't know what we were going to do. We were trying to get our cooking merit badge, Andy and I thought if we told our Scoutmaster that our ten pounds of hotdogs had been spoiled we might be kicked out of the troop. So what we did was get some hot water and we cleaned the slime off the hotdogs. Then we decided to find a big iron skillet from one of the other troops. We were going to boil the hotdogs, but decided to dice up the dogs and fry them up and no one would know the difference. If there were any bacteria or anything wrong with the dogs it'd be killed in the frying pan. And we did and every one thought the meal was wonderful. Nobody got sick and we got our cooking merit badge and everybody was happy.

By this time my mother and father were allowing me to travel by bicycle to other sections of the city. I'd work the circuses and also visit my cousin Donald in the North End. Now he lives in Baltimore and is retired. When my mother went to visit her sister she'd always take me. Donald and I would play along the tracks. He lived right across from the railroad station on Deer Street. Our biggest enjoyment was walking up the tracks to the roundhouse. The roundhouse was about half a mile up the tracks and that's where all the engines were taken in to be worked on—the big, huge steam engines. It was like driving a car over a pit for changing your oil. The trains would be over a pit and the engineers would be under the engines pulling big wheels and big pistons off. We'd stand in the doorway and watch them. It was hard work, but it was fascinating to watch. Sometimes they'd have two or three engines in the roundhouse. We'd be there for every train that came in. Part of the roundhouse is gone now. It was up near the Button Factory.

One thing I always remember is that my aunt Olive catered to the hoboes that got off the train. When the train came in, the hoboes would know where the free handouts were, because there was a cross on the riser section of the steps. The railroad station was directly across the street from the where my aunt lived and, when the hoboes got off the boxcars where they slept and rode, they would look around at all the houses lined up on Deer Street. When they saw a cross marked in chalk on a riser they knew they could knock on the door and they'd get a handout. Sure enough, I'd hear the train come in and within five minutes there'd be a knock on the door. My mother, my aunt, Donnie, and I would be having lunch, and my aunt would go to the door. She always had pastries on the kitchen table. There'd be pies, homemade cookies, and brownies and she'd put pieces in a paper bag. She'd always say, "Poor soul, poor soul." She never would talk about it. I don't know why, but once I took a rag and brushed off the white chalk cross. I didn't really know what it was. I thought someone was vandalizing the house. My cousin found out and told me why that cross was there and to never, ever do that again.

When I got into the eighth grade I was still studying a lot, still trying to keep my marks up, but my report cards were Cs and Ds. If I did get an A —I got it in woodshop—I was given something like 25 cents. That was a lot of money.

There was one little girl by the name of Carol who lived right besides the Haven playground and she used to help me with my homework. I always went by her house when I was taking my bike out. We talked. She was the same age as I was and she was brilliant.

In 1939 I knew (Franklin Delano) Roosevelt was president because my mother took me downtown to see him come by train and be motorcaded down Daniel Street to go to the Shipyard for a meeting. I'll never forget standing on the corner of Daniel and Pleasant at Market Square and his motorcade passed right by me. I saw Roosevelt in the back of an open car with his hat and his cigar holder. Just like he always did.

We weren't reading the paper, just the funnies and the sports section. Headlines were means of selling papers. Sometimes I had four or five papers left over from my route. That was a luxury. I'd rush downtown to sell them and make a profit. Instead of counting out 120 papers—whoever was doing it might count out 124,125—and I had those extras. That was extra money in my pocket—total profit. I'd try to catch the Navy Yard traffic coming off the Shipyard by bus and car off the Shipyard. Busses came down Daniel Street and cars came down State. When a car came from the Shipyard it was with five passengers—I never saw just a single person in a car, because they had to carpool.

I had a few extra papers one time and wanted to pick the prime corner to get rid of these six or seven extra papers. I decided on the corner of Pleasant and State, which is right by the old Post Office. They'd have to stop by the lights there and continue down State. That was an ideal spot to sell papers. But I had horned in on another guy's corner. His name was Jackson and he told me, "Hey, buddy, kid, what are you doing here?" And I said, "I'm taking over." And he said, "You are, huh?" and he hit me on the nose and knocked me on the ground. My papers went all over the place and blood was all over the papers. I didn't say a word and scooped the papers up and took off. That's a no-no, taking over somebody else's corner for selling newspapers. I should have known better. I tried to act bold but I couldn't bluff him. He was tough, the toughest guy from the North End.

An 1890 view of Pleasant and State Streets where a youghful Harold attempted to sell nrwspapers in another boy's territory.

I turned thirteen in July of 1941. I remember how hot that summer was because we had a jellyfish fight. I'd like to explain about these jellyfish that we collected at the South Mill Pond. Along the millpond there were many things that ate up the algae there from the direct sewer line that dumped into the pond—horseshoe crabs, jellyfish, groupies, and minnows. We used to have a lot of fun with the horseshoe crabs we brought home, but my mother convinced me that once that tail shot up and it stung you, you only had minutes to live because they were considered poisonous. I believed that so I brought no more horseshoe crabs home.

But about the jellyfish: the tide was unusually low during one period and it left a lot of live and dead jellyfish along the shore. This was right near where we used to play along the cliff area, which is off South Street and directly behind the old Portsmouth Hospital. My friend Donald and I went down there one day, and we picked up the jellyfish, looked at them, and then he threw one at me and I threw one at him and then an idea came up. "Let's collect these jellyfish and have a jellyfish fight." So we went home and got a basket and we collected half a bushel of jellyfish. We collected probably fifty of them. These were white jellyfish. And then the news went around the neighborhood where there were a lot of kids that there was going to be a jellyfish fight at two o'clock in the afternoon at the

The wooden bridge to Peirce Island where Harold and his friends swam.

Haven School playground.

Come two o'clock, we took the jellyfish from the basket and who-ever wanted to join us could. We divided ourselves up into two teams— probably eight or nine boys on each team. The girls stood around the play-ground watching us. We gave each other one jellyfish for each hand and we lined up and charged each other with a "1, 2, 3 go." We had our shirts off and it was almost 100 degrees and we loved the jellyfish hitting us in our face and on our bodies because it cooled us off.

But there were broken up pieces of jellyfish in this dirt and gravel area that wasn't part of the hot-topped playground. The only part of the playground that was hot-topped was the basketball court. The rest of the playground was all dirt and gravel and it started smelling. The next day somebody complained and they sent public works down to look it over. Before the end of the day, they sent down a fire truck to hose everything off. They wanted to know what happened and all of us kids were, "We know nothing, we know nothing." It was an ungodly smell and it went throughout the whole neighborhood. That smell stayed in that dirt for quite a while during that summer.

We swam all over the place that summer. Not only at Peirce Island, but also under the bridge going to Peirce Island, which was much more exciting because the tide came in and there were little rapids. We swam off the Peirce Island Bridge too. This is not the bridge that is there now. The old bridge had pillars along the walkway and we used to shimmy up the pillars. I didn't. The pillars were only about a foot in diameter and you'd shimmy up and then do a sailor's dive off the top of the pillars. My friend Kenny would always do a sailor's dive, which is when you keep your hands close to your waist and hit the water like a rocket.

We used to swim off Memorial Bridge—not the center, but off to one side. We'd have a rowboat, waiting for us and we'd do a sailor's dive. I wouldn't do it but I'd be around collecting money in a hat from the people who'd gather around to see a sailor's dive. Then the attendant came down from his Control House, where he was also attending the gate of the Memorial Bridge, and chased us away. It was an attraction, a way of making some money. I'd get 50 or 75 cents in nickels and pennies and we'd split it amongst ourselves.

We swam at the Slide, which was a place at Pleasant Point that was off Newcastle Avenue. It was undeveloped down there and we called it The Slide because there was a rock formation and at high tide you could slide down into the water on a piece of cardboard. We also swam at Ridge's Court. We had all these places that we knew where to go, but that nobody else in the city did. This was strictly for South Enders.

We'd also go out to Lafayette Road, where WHEB-FM and the Dinnerhorn are now. That was quite a ways out for us. We'd ride our bikes out on old Route 1, where was an old bridge over Sagamore Creek. There was good swimming there in a hole that at high tide was probably twenty or twenty-five feet deep.

My brother and I would go fishing a lot. We'd go with a drop line down at the first Newcastle Bridge, and we'd come home with a basketful of flounder in less than an hour. We'd buy five cents worth of worms at

Down's Store. It was a lot of fun, but my mother would get so upset because we would bring home so much flounder. "I'm not cleaning any more flounder for you children. Don't bring any more home." We'd take them down to a big family of six down the street.

Begging down at the bakeries and at the back of the restaurants down town was another activity for us. On a Saturday afternoon we'd go knocking on the doors of two baker's shops down on Daniel Street and a restaurant there called Thorner's, and ask if they had any day old pastry. There'd be four or five of us kids and they'd always send me up to knock on the door because I was the skinniest and I looked the poorest. I always had old shoes on and a runny nose and looked shaggy. I'd say, "Do you have any day-old pastry?" and the cook would look at me and say, "I'll be right back." He'd come back and have a bag full of donuts and éclairs and parfaits that were two or three days old. We'd do this at two or three restaurants too. Our best restaurant was behind the Rockingham Hotel on Porter Street. We knew where the back door of the restaurant was and we'd bang on it until somebody came. We always got some goodies there.

Then the four or five of us would take the bag of pastries and ride our bikes up to The Pines, that was located off South Street, in the back of what is now Edgewood Manor. This was about a fifty-acre area between South Street and Jones Avenue that we South Enders tried to claim as our own recreational area. Other neighborhoods eventually found out about the place and it became Portsmouth's recreation area. People hiked and camped in the summer and during the winter there was a toboggan run and a small walk-up-the-hill ski jump. With tall pines, oaks, and birches, it was a beautiful place. The scattered ledge out crops were ideal for lean-tos, made from pine boughs and sticks, and hide outs. We'd get under a lean-to and have our feast on a Saturday afternoon when we didn't go to the movies.

But going to the movies was a big thing, too. There were three theaters downtown: The Olympia, The Arcadia, and The Colonial. The Colonial was where the best features were shown and was the most expensive. It was fifteen cents to go to the movies there, whereas the others were nine and ten cents; nine cents in the afternoon at the Arcadia Theater and ten cents in the evening. The Olympia Theater was on Vaughan Street, where the Vaughan Mall is now, one block down from Congress.

The Arcadia Theater, which we called "the Scratch House," was located on the Franklin Block. For nine cents you could see a feature, a secondary movie, Paramount News, a serial, and two or three cartoons.

OLYMPIA THEATRE PORTSMOUTH

CONTINUOUS WEEKDAYS 1:30-11:00 P. M.

CONTINUOUS SUNDAYS 6:00-11:00 P. M.

1941   MARCH   1941

SUN.	MON.	TUE.	WED.	THUR.	FRI.	SAT.
2	3	4	5	6	7	8

5 DAYS! The Greatest Motion Picture of All Time! "GONE WITH THE WIND" starring CLARK GABLE, VIVIEN LEIGH, LESLIE HOWARD, OLIVIA de HAVILAND
One Show Only Sunday Eve at 7:00 P. M. — Monday thru Thursday Two Shows at 1:30 and 7:30 P. M.

Bill BOYD "IN OLD COLORADO" THE MARX BROS. in "GO WEST"
Cartoon Comedy ... Latest News

| 9 | 10 | 11 | 12 | 13 | 14 | 15 |

GARY COOPER in "Northwest Mounted Police" with Madeleine Carroll, Paulette Goddard, Robert Preston
Hugh Herbert and Big Fun Cast in "Meet The Chump"

BETTE DAVIS in "THE LETTER" with Herbert Marshall, James Stephenson
"Ride, Kelly, Ride" - Eugene Pallette

PAUL MUNI in "HUDSON'S BAY" Charles Butterworth, Virginia Grey
"BLONDE INSPIRATION"

| 16 | 17 | 18 | 19 | 20 | 21 | 22 |

ALICE FAYE in "TIN PAN ALLEY" with JACK OAKIE, BETTY GRABLE, JOHN PAYNE
LLOYD NOLAN, LYNN BARI in "SLEEPERS WEST"

139 STARS! 1000 THRILLS! "LAND OF LIBERTY"
Henry Fonda, Dorothy Lamour-"Chad Hanna"

"THE THIEF OF BAGDAD" In Color! with SABU, CONRAD VEIDT
"Mr. Dynamite" with Lloyd Nolan

| 23 | 24 | 25 | 26 | 27 | 28 | 29 |

Errol Flynn, Olivia deHaviland in "Santa Fe Trail"
ROBERT MONTGOMERY, INGRID BERGMAN GEORGE SANDERS in "RAGE IN HEAVEN"

JOAN BLONDELL, DICK POWELL in "MODEL WIFE"
John Wayne in "Long Voyage Home"

Charlie Chan in "Dead Men Tell" CLARK GABLE, HEDY LAMARR in "COMRADE X"

CONSOLIDATION COAL COMPANY

35 Pleasant Street   ▲   J. C. SHAW, Manager   ▲   Opposite Post Office

We Handle only the Best Grade of Hard Coal, Soft Coal and New England Coke

Phone 90   "You'll Like Our Service"

Coming attractions posters were given out each month.

Probably four hours of entertainment at the movie house.

We'd buy popcorn at Newberry's for ten cents, a big bag of popcorn we could all share. But the Scratch House was a dirty theater. After the lights went out you could hear scampering across the floor. We didn't say anything, but we knew that there were little mice and little rats running across the floor. That's why we called it the Scratch House. We'd always come back week after week because of the serials. The villain would be thrown off the cliff and the movie would stop and we'd come back the next week and the villain that had been thrown off the cliff would land in a bag of feathers and he would be saved, or something like that.

I'll never forget the time we sneaked into the movies. I was about 15 years old and didn't have enough money to get in. So we devised a plan where we diverted the attention of the usher. One of us had enough money to get into the theater and, as we went upstairs to give the ticket to the usher, we'd start talking to him and would sneak behind him through the doors so he wouldn't notice us.

At the Olympia Theater I attempted to sneak in, but I got caught. The manager took me right down to his office and had a talk with me. What frightened me was that he sat me down and he opened his wallet and showed me an auxiliary police badge. That frightened me to death. I promised him I would never, ever try to sneak in again. He said he wouldn't contact my mother and father as long as I came back and talked to him every afternoon after school for a period of one whole week and told him what I did in school. I did that and I never sneaked in the movies again. All he had to do was show me that badge and say he wasn't going to tell my mother and father and that convinced me.

You couldn't smoke in the theaters in Portsmouth. You could in the theaters of the larger cities, like Boston or New York, but I never knew anybody to smoke while seated. They smoked in the entranceway and in the men's room and in the lobby, but the women didn't smoke at all, they wouldn't be seen smoking.

I liked the westerns. Tom Mix, Buck Jones, the Lone Ranger, and, Gene Autry were my favorites.

Once in a while we'd see vaudeville. I'd go with my mother and they'd give dishes away. My mother loved the movies and she'd drag me from one theater to and other. We'd go late in the afternoon and go late at night, three different theaters in one day.

My mother loved vaudeville. We'd see any vaudeville act available. We'd see dog acts or pigeon acts. The pigeons would fly around, and would float down on this guy's hands. We'd see somebody who could ride a unicycle or a bicycle and do tricks or anybody who could do juggling. I mean, it was entertainment, but today, people wouldn't accept this type of entertainment. But in those days a juggling act, a magician act, a trick-riding bicyclist, or a unicyclist, were all novel and funny to us. Slapstick comedy also was a big thing.

There was another kind of entertainment and it had to do with rats. My friend Donald got a BB gun, a Daisy Air Rifle, for his birthday. For something exciting to do we'd go to the Jones Avenue dump, throw a big boulder down on the rubbish pile, and out would come the rats because they thought another load was being dumped. We would stand at the top of the pile of rubbish and shoot down at the rats. Some of them were as big

Harold and his friends used to shoot rats along Newcastle Avenue shore. Courtesy Portsmouth Athenaeum.

as cats and we'd hit them and it wouldn't even faze them. They wouldn't even stop munching on the garbage. I didn't have an air rifle; my mother would never allow me to have one. I had a nice long slingshot made out of two pieces of cut inner tube strands tied together. I used marbles most of the time, small marbles, and they would hurt. I made the slingshot myself out of stiff wire. So we'd go down to the Jones Avenue dump with the BB gun and the slingshot and spend a summer afternoon.

We'd also go down to the Newcastle Avenue seawall when the tide went out. That was before you got to the bridges to New Castle and where the people dumped their garbage overboard thinking this was the thing to do because when the tide went out and it took the garbage with it and we understood that you were feeding the fish, helping the marine life. Dumping overboard your old tomatoes and cabbages and radishes and things that rotted, things you weren't able to get out of the ground fast enough from the garden.

The rats lived under the seawall and they'd come out at low tide and munch on garbage that wasn't taken out by the tide. And we'd go down and stand by the railing and shoot our BB gun and slingshot at them. So this was a day or afternoon of entertainment, we'd be there for hours shooting at rats.

When it was hot like it was that summer I slept in the hallway. In my bedroom in the attic it was ungodly hot. With one little window, the temperature got to 80 or 90 degrees. My mother would allow my brother and me to take our blankets to the second floor hallway where the breeze went through and it was much cooler because it was away from the hot attic.

People slept on the porch—if you had one—or a piazza. If you had a tent in the back yard, you'd sleep in the tent. I did that a couple of times.

When I was delivering the *Portsmouth Herald* there was a promotion. If you got five new subscribers you could go to Boston and see the Red Sox and stay over at the YMCA. It was a big deal. I got my new subscribers and I think there were two carloads of paperboys that got five new customers. That was an honor. My mother gave her consent and Richie, from the circulation department at the *Herald,* took us down. We saw the Red Sox game in the afternoon and then we went to the YMCA where we were assigned a certain bed in a big dorm-type room with fifty-five or sixty cots in it. Everybody came out of the playroom where there were pool tables and ping-pong tables and card tables and games that you could play. Come ten o'clock the alarm went off for everybody to get into bed.

Well, the lights went out and I wanted to have a good time. There I was away from home and it was pitch dark except for the little red lights where the exits were. I would crawl on my hands and knees four or five bunks down and pull the covers off somebody's bed and run back fast. There would be commotion and the councilors would come in from their room and turn on the light and want to know what happened. I did this four or five times and they gave a warning: "Stop your fooling, you kids." They didn't know who it was until I got caught. They put the light on when I was crawling down again.

You know what the councilors had me do? They took me down to the boiler room —he warned me he was going to do it but I thought it was a big joke—and I had to shovel coal into the furnace. It was about 120 degrees in the boiler room. I went back to my bunk and I didn't do anything else after that, I learned my lesson. The counselor came back to the *Herald* and told the circulation director about me. I never tried to get in on a promotion again because I thought I would never be allowed.

A Dark side of Portsmouth

One day I was visiting my cousin Donald in the North End when it was raining. We were visiting another house on Deer Street and decided to play Monopoly, but we couldn't find the Monopoly set. This friend of ours said I think I know where the Monopoly set is and he went to his father's desk,

The Portsmouth Ku Klux Klan meeting at Brackett Field, above and opposite page.

got the key and went up to the attic. They kept their attic locked and there was a winding little stairway to get up there. There were rickety floors, all dirty, one little light. We were looking around through some boxes for the Monopoly set. I saw way over in the corner a sheet hanging with a pointed headdress. I went over to my friend and said, "I didn't know your father went out on Halloween." He didn't answer me. Finally, his mother heard us up in the attic; "You kids come down from there right now! I'm telling you you're not supposed to be up in that attic!" But when we got downstairs I said to my friend's mother, "Gee, I didn't know Mr. ... went out at Halloween time. I'd like to have him make me one of those costumes, just like he's got up there." She said, "When you visit this house don't you ever go up in that attic. Give me the key and never unlock that door again." Later on in life I found out he was a member of the Portsmouth Ku Klux Klan. I didn't realize that until I was much older.

My mother sometimes told me, back in 1938 and '39, "Don't go down to Brackett Field," which was only a short distance from my house. She would say, "Don't go down there this weekend because there's a church service going on. It's going to be both Saturday and Sunday." Brackett Field is where the Little Harbour School is now and it was an open field then. My mother would never tell us about the KKK meetings or anything like that.

In 1928, '29, and '30 there was a fairly active KKK in Portsmouth.

Someone told me several years ago that everyone who went down there with a hood on would say, Hi, Sam, Hi, Joe, Hi, Mike. How are you? Everybody knew everybody, yet they all wore a hood. By the 1940s, the Klan had just about disbanded in Portsmouth.

Chapter Three: The War Years

September 1941

In the eighth grade we took a subject called geography. We were shown where Poland and Czechoslovakia were and brought up to date on what Germany was doing. We knew the Germans invaded Czechoslovakia, and we knew what the Nazis were. We followed it fairly close, but all of us kids figured it was so far away. We'd look at the globe and turn it around and see where the United States was, at the farther end of the world, and it wasn't of much interest to us.

Dec. 7, 1941

December 7th was a beautiful Sunday. I had been out playing baseball in the playground with my friends. I think the temperature was in the 40s—bright sun so we came in at four o'clock. It was a routine to listen to our favorite program, which was "The Shadow." We all gathered around the radio, about four of us, and halfway through the program it was interrupted to announce the sneak attack. We didn't even know where Pearl Harbor was and I was just upset because they interrupted "The Shadow." I kept moving the dial to another station to see if we could get the program again and finally we went back to the station and the program continued. We didn't know where Pearl Harbor was or what the issue was. We didn't take it seriously. Mother and father had gone out for a ride with the rest of the family; it was just my brother Bobby and I at home.

It was very, very quiet at dinner. We listened to the radio; we got all our news from the radio. It was from then on that everybody talked about the war and the war effort and everybody became very patriotic. Every move you made was toward the war effort. We started collecting aluminum foil from cigarette packages. If we opened a package very carefully, we could tear off this foil and make balls as big as a football and then somebody came and collected it. We collected string and rags, and all kinds of brass and copper.

The South End was changing. It changed right after Pearl Harbor. That's when many, many people came to this city to work at Portsmouth Naval Shipyard.

And then there came the draft and that's when my father worried and got us all together and told us he probably would have to go, that his number would be coming up pretty soon. But every time his number came up they found out he had six children. He was working at the Shipyard and he had an essential job. Right before the war started he was transferred to an electrical job and worked on the submarines as an electrician's helper on the boats and pulled cable through the wire ways. He worked real hard on the diesel boats. It was six days a week and then seven days a week, sometimes ten or twelve hours a day.

In Portsmouth, especially the South End, a lot of people had been coming to work at the Shipyard, which went from about 9,000 employees to 24,000 employees during 1942. Men were coming in—single men, or men with just a wife and no children—looking for rooms. Sometimes both the wife and the husband would be employed at the Shipyard. People were renting upstairs rooms, a room at the back of the house, or a room out over the garage. Any space where people could sleep and use a hotplate to cook their meals was rented.

Things changed even in the house we were living in. It was a double house, we rented the front part and the back section had six rooms like we had, but the family there only had three people. So they had plenty of space to rent upstairs and rented to two men who were working at the Shipyard. They came and went as they wanted to, and cooked their meals on a hot plate in their room. Most of their meals were eaten at the restaurant on the Shipyard. They mingled right in as if they were family and this happened all over the South End. In fact, it happened all over the city. Rooming houses and boarding houses were filled up. There were no motels; there were hotels, but they were too expensive for Shipyard workers to stay in. Downtown there was the Rockingham Hotel, the Kearsage, and the DeWitt Hotel, but they were very expensive.

Portsmouth became a very patriotic city in that short period of time. The Shipyard was launching submarines every sixty to ninety days. Many times my father came home from work and said there was going to be a launching, I made it a point to either get out of school early or, if it was a Saturday, to finish my paper route early, and watch that launching. My brother and I loved to go over to Peirce Island and see that. There also were two detachments of Marines stationed at the Marine barracks on the Shipyard—the oldest Marine barracks in the nation. We also had the Coast Guard at New Castle patrolling our harbors—active all the time.

The Coast Artillery was being trained at the National Guard Armory on Parrott Avenue, and they manned the forts at Odiorne Point in Rye, Fort McClary in Kittery, and Fort Constitution in New Castle to protect our harbor; we all thought the enemy was right off the coast. Then there was the Army National Guard that was activated in 1940 and they served very honorably. By the middle of 1942, we were frightened that Portsmouth could be attacked.

People talked about the war every place we went. In the schools, we had to read for Civics class the headlines about what was happening in Germany, in Japan, and the Pacific. We read about the Pacific islands where the Marines were taking control. In downtown on a Saturday morning or a Friday night, people congregated and talked. The armory had USO dances, celebrities from Hollywood come in by train, and they had war bond drives where just about half the city would line up. There would be a long line of people down Parrott Avenue waiting to buy an $18.75 war bond that would be worth $25 after the war ended. We would save the money we got for lunch and buy war bond stamps and we got the book filled.

To jump ahead a little ways, I remember servicemen coming back in 1945 and at the Armory there was a big ceremony. The whole city came out and ribbons and awards and medals were given to the National Guard Armory unit that served in the war

At the movies, Paramount news was the first thing we saw— the latest of what was happening. We were rationed, that was almost immediate. By the middle of 1942 we were given ration stamps and we could only buy a certain amount of meat, or butter, or cooking oil a month. There was one other item that was very scarce and that was gasoline. My father had an "A" sticker. There were "A," "B," and "C." "C" was mostly for commercial vehicles, and not for residential and private operating vehicles, but my father was given a little extra gas because he was always taking passengers back and forth from the Navy Yard.

We had these playing cards that we got from bubble gum and on the cards all the planes were identified that belonged to Germany and Japan. We'd play games and hold the cards up for just a second and we had to tell the specifics about a German plane or a Japanese Zero, how fast they went or what kind of armament they had—you knew the statistics.

These cards were issued every month in the lobby at the movie theaters and were free and you went in the first or second day of the month and picked them up. The cards told what the movies were and who was playing in them. Everybody went for those cards and I still have one from 1940 and one from 1941.

There were no Japanese people in town that I can remember. There were two or three Chinese families that had been here before the war. I don't remember any German families. We heard about larger cities, like in California, where people were afraid of spies mingling among us. Because the bombing of Pearl Harbor had been so secretive—it happened without anybody knowing about it—the whole country figured people who were giving information back to Japan or Germany were jeopardizing our national security.

We were told there were secret agents and no one kind of trusted anybody. But in Portsmouth it was strictly patriotic, military. "Loose lips sink ships" was one of the slogans. That was the first thing we saw in a newsreel when we went to the movies. At the age of fourteen I was appointed assistant air raid warden for my section of the city. So here we were in the year 1943 and I was turning fourteen years old in the middle of the summer. In the fall I would go into my first year of high school as a freshman.

That summer my father's number again came up in the draft. My mother called us all together and told us that I might be taking over and that I would be the man of the house. I said, "Ma, I'm only fourteen." "Well," she said, "If dad goes into the Army you've got to help us keep the family together—keep your brothers and sisters from getting into trouble. You are the oldest."

My father went down to the draft board and was interviewed. They found out again—for the second time—that he had six children under sixteen years old and he was thirty-five years old. The limit on the draft was 18 to 36; he was right at the edge of that age limit. Also, he worked at the Shipyard building submarines. So that was all the criteria he needed for deferment. He was never called up again. This was in the summer of 1943, at the height of the war.

Draftees were leaving by the hundreds. We would go down to the railroad station every other Saturday morning and see another group of draftees leaving by train, going to Fort Drum in New York for training. The band would be playing, the mayor would be down there, flags waving, and all the draftees—maybe thirty or forty of them, would be given small ditty bags. In the bag there'd be a shaving kit, a bar of soap, toothpaste, a tooth-brush, and a little packet of cigarettes, with six in the package. The ditty bag was made of canvas with a drawstring at the top. Mayor Mary C. Dondero made sure the draftees got on the train with a real gigantic send off.

There were a lot of families affected by the war, especially in the South End. We noticed banners hanging in the windows, Blue Star families, one, or two, or three stars. That meant there were three members in the family in the Marines, the Navy, or the Army. One family we knew very well on Marcy Street had four sons in the military. Hermie was one of my best friends and all his brothers were in the military. They were strong, patriotic people, and Hermie and I couldn't wait to come of age so we could volunteer ourselves. In fact, later five us would go down to the recruiting office begging to get in, begging, but if you were under age you had to get your parent's permission.

The Army draftees left from the railroad station down on Deer Street and went to Fort Drum in New York. The Marines left by van and went to Manchester. The Navy would go by bus either to Bainbridge, Maryland, or the Great Lakes Naval Training Station in Illinois.

There was great fanfare, with mothers and fathers crying, but very patriotic. Every so often we'd see a gold star hanging from a banner in a window and that would mean a soldier or a Marine or a sailor had been killed. We kids would always be quiet and never play in front of those houses. It was very solemn and we took it very seriously. We made sure those driveways were shoveled out during the winter season, or we'd find an old lawn mower at one of the houses and make sure their lawn was mowed without saying a word. My mother would say many times, "You take this pot of beans and bring it down the street. They just lost their dad, or their son, in the war." She'd make homemade bread. "Take this hot bread and if they are not there, just leave it on the steps."

The first person in the South End I remember being killed in the war was a Marine. He went in when he was seventeen. He quit school and was killed on one of the Japanese Islands. Ronnie was his first name. It was sad, very sad. Ronnie always wanted to be a Marine.

The whole city was buzzing with military activity. The submarines were coming in for repair from out on patrol. The sailors were downtown. Marine battalions were over at the barracks at the Shipyard. There weren't many Army personnel because they were all stationed at the forts around Portsmouth, at the coast artillery living in barracks.

In the downtown there were sixty-five or seventy beer joints as we called them. Those beer joints were buzzing with activity on a weekend, especially when a submarine was in. Some of the bars were Roger's, the Starlight, Leary's, the Club Café, and the Golden Horseshoe. They were scattered throughout the city, every side street, every main street, State Street, Daniel Street, High Street—all of them had a beer joint.

There were only two private clubs in Portsmouth that served liquor, but most of the military didn't patronize them. One was the Forest Club and the other was called the Fleet Reserve Club. You had to buy a membership and you could go in and get liquor. But the military guys wanted strictly beer, draft beer or bottled beer.

Prior to World War II, entertainment in the downtown district was limited. Movies and bowling were the main escapes in this depressed city. I would join my father for routine Saturday morning chores and I would often hear, "Hey, Joe," "Hey, Mike, what have you got on your hip?" If there was a movement of body English or a hand patting the back pocket that was an indication that Joe or Mike would share their last swig from a pint of cheap whiskey. So down the nearest alley they'd go. Occasionally someone would share a gallon of wine he'd hidden behind some trash-cans. Often a fist fight would break out over something minor, ending as quickly as it started, the two fighters then buying each other a beer in one of the joints. People from other sections of the city would often refer to those folks as, "those old South Enders!"

There were only a few restaurants downtown. One was Jarvis's Restaurant, another was Steve's, and there was the Clipper, and Thorner's Oyster House on Daniel Street. But that was it. At Steve's they cooked in the window. Everybody loved to hang around and watch the cook fry hamburgers, or steaks, or ham and eggs—right in the window. Steve's was right on Congress Street where the Friendly Toast is now. The Clipper Restaurant—the building has been torn down—was located where the Eagle Photo parking lot was.

At the armory, every Saturday morning, all of us kids would watch the Coast Guard Artillery drill. They had a large gun over there. The drill was a mock up—they never fired the gun. We heard one day they were going to haul that big five-inch howitzer down to Rye Beach and fire it off shore. The Coast Guard was towing a target. So we got on our bikes and went down to the old Coast Guard station at Wallis Sands and sat on the wall. The Coast Guard station was located just south of Wallis Sands

National Guard Armory, later the JFK Center, on Parrott Avenue was torn down to make way for the new city library.

Beach. Wallis Sands was like a no man's land. It wasn't a state beach then and only natives went down there. All sand dunes and rocks, it wasn't a good beach to go to until after the war when it was made into a beautiful state beach.

We sat and watched that big five-inch gun fired off. The road was blocked off and nobody could go down that road while they were practicing. They fired shells five miles out to sea on a towed bulls-eye target. We never saw them hit it, but they came close. And then we went to New Castle where they brought back the target and it was just as new as the day they took it out, but they came close.

The Coast Artillery was at the armory. In 1944, there was so much military and so much patriotism in the city of Portsmouth, it was really unbelievable. Marines, sailors, Army soldiers, jeeps, rack trucks, and two-and-a-half-ton trucks were going up and down Sagamore and South Streets, through down town, heading toward Fort Dearborn down in New Castle, toward Odiorne's Point in Rye, or to Fort Foster in Kittery. There was the downtown shore patrol working with the local police on a Saturday night. There were sailors and Marines in the different bars.

The paper route I took in the morning caused me to be late for school several mornings so, after the winter was over, my mother made me give it up. It was too much. I had the Boy Scouts, work at the *Herald* on the mailing bench after school, my paper route, and the Demolay. I was finding it difficult to study for school and keep up my marks.

At fifteen I entered the new brick high school downtown. I found it really interesting going into a huge building. We South Enders would always gather in the morning at seven o'clock and walk to school together. We'd go up Pleasant Street and down through the city and into the high school. We had picked a course in our freshman year at the junior high where the freshman classes were held. We entered the high school in our sophomore year and I chose the mechanical arts course because it meant a lot of shop training.

In my sophomore year I took mechanical drawing, shop math, and electricity. My basic courses were English, history, and civics. Some of the shop teachers were Linscott, Hargreaves, and Mr. Malloy who taught drafting. Mr. C.C. Sandborn was the principal of the school. Some of the teachers who taught the academic studies were Miss Flanagan, Miss Brady, and Miss Ballard—all those teachers made a lasting impression on us students. We always remembered something about them that kind of stayed in our minds after we got out of high school and went on in life.

The teachers were very strict, but kind and concerned because many of them knew that we came from the South End, the poor section of the city. They were very aware of our poor status, our clothing, and that we came from large families and were not able to have the best of things.

I'll never forget one project that we had. Mr. Hargreaves was looking for volunteers to go into the attic and clean up. The attic had a lot of electrical cable, old switches, transformers, and light fixtures that were strewn all over the place and had to be cleaned up and put in boxes and stored. We had to take a little narrow stairway to get up to the attic. Louie and I volunteered and we stayed up there one whole semester—six weeks. And we got an "A" in electricity for that semester.

I was amazed at the construction of that old yellow brick building. In the attic I climbed up a ladder to the cupolas, where I could look out. There are two cupolas up there and the view is amazing—I could see the whole city—Memorial Bridge—the entire downtown. I saw all the outlying areas. There were only two bridges at that time. The middle bridge was built in 1940, but the Route I-95 Bridge wasn't built until the early 1970s.

It was amazing that I could see Wentworth Acres; it had finally been completed. This was a government housing project and it was huge. It had rentals for more than 800 people and it was mostly for the Shipyard workers. I could see Pannaway Manor, out on Sherburne Road, which was another government housing project. I never realized how huge these projects were. There were little houses out in Pannaway, but at Wentworth Acres there were duplexes, triplexes, and some single houses. Wentworth Acres was the same place where Osprey Landing is now (called Spinnaker Point) off in the northern part of the city.

For cleaning up the attic they had to give us coveralls and gloves because it was so dirty. We cleaned and we boxed everything, and they came up and inspected afterwards and thought it was wonderful. I did get to carve my initials up there. We all carried pocketknives and I carved my initials in the beams way up in the rafters. I climbed the ladder and every day I did a little more on my initials, "Whitey, Class of 46." Today when the Portsmouth Housing Authority goes up to do an inspection on the old high school, now an elderly housing project, called the Keefe House, they shine the light up to check the beams to see if there is any roof leakage. Sure enough, they see my name up there and always comment to me about it. "How did you get up there and how was it done and why has it lasted so long.' I carved it deep in those huge, 14- by 14-inch beams.

In 1944, we were getting older and were watching the progress of the war more closely. We'd gather on a stormy Sunday afternoon at someone's house, eight or ten of us—spread out at the kitchen table and help one another in math or the sciences or history. I had tremendous trouble in English. We'd also talk about the war and about someone who had been drafted and was getting ready to go, and where someone we knew was in the military.

We all looked up to the president. We thought Franklin Delano Roosevelt was one of our finest presidents. We listened to his fireside chats on the radio. My mother and father demanded that we all gather around and these chats were in the early part of the evening and would bring us up to date on the war. We all had to be quiet and the radio would fade out and come back again—we had this old radio—but we always took such interest in his talk.

One summer Saturday my father asked me if I would like to go over to the Shipyard and get right close to a launching of one of the submarines. So I rode my bike over to the pass office and my father met me and took me over to what was called the hill, the building ways. I often wondered what the hill was like. My father would come home and say, "Up on the hill was hot today" if it was in the summer, or, "Up on the hill was cold today" if it was in the winter. So I always wondered what the hill was like.

The Shipyard was a heavily guarded place. It wasn't easy to get into. There were 24,000 workers there—8,000 workers to a shift. Marines guarded the gates. My father had to go in and get a pass for me, had to verify who I was, and had to stay with me until I was in the building ways. It was strictly a secured place. It was not patrolled in the river, but secured if you had to go through the gates.

So he took me up on the hill and said to me, "You stand right here. See the black hull of the submarine? It's going to go down the ways in about one hour." So, I was all by myself and I stood there, and my father said, "Don't you move. I have to go back to work." There was nobody around me. About a half-hour before the sub was launched, people started coming in, and started pushing me back. I was just a little shaver, I only weighed about ninety-five pounds, and I couldn't see. I heard speeches, I heard the band play, and I heard the Shipyard whistle go and all I saw go by me were the flags that were decorating the submarine. That was it. All the people left, and I was there by myself when my father came back to get me, and he said, "It was very exciting, wasn't it?" And I said, "Dad, I thought it was exciting." I never told him I thought it was the most boring thing I have ever witnessed. From now on I decided to watch the submarines being launched from Peirce Island. He thought he was doing me a big favor.

They were launching a submarine every sixty to seventy days. They would bring up a group of submarine sailors from sub school in Groton, Connecticut to man these subs. They were young kids and they were kind of sowing their oats before they went out to sea. They knew that sub service was very dangerous. They called it the Silent Service. When they were out on patrol they'd stay six to eight months without coming back into port—if they did come back—we lost many subs out there in World War II.

A sense we're winning the war

All the military who were coming back in the summer of 1944 said we were winning the war. We'd see them with their ribbons on and they'd gather us round and talk to us. We'd hear that so-and-so was back in town and we'd go and knock on the door. We love to hear the stories and they always brought us back souvenirs—a Japanese item from one of the islands or something from the German Army.

I was thinking about becoming a sailor at this point, but my mother would always tell us to stay away from any side streets or downtown places where there were many beer joints. "If you go downtown stay right on Congress Street," she'd say. "Don't you dare venture down Daniel Street, Market Street, Penhallow, or any of the side streets where the beer joints are." Drinking or smoking was never allowed in my house, and we were always close to the church.

My father was now working seven days a week. By this time we were starting to have a few things. My mother was buying us clothes through Sears & Roebuck and Spiegel's catalogues. Downtown there was J.J. Newberry's and Grant's where you could buy accessories. There were a couple of clothing stores for suits, but they were very expensive for children. You could also go into Montgomery Wards and buy through the catalogue.

She was still picking up things at the Goodwill, but we were looking a little bit better with our clothing. We were able to take vacations each summer up to the mountains camping.

My gang of South End friends was really close by this time. This wasn't a gang out looking for trouble; we helped one another, especially in our schoolwork, and in our problems. We went to the movies together on a Saturday night, a group of six, seven, eight of us—but there was one thing; I had to be home when the curfew sounded. No matter what kind of a movie it was, or if I hadn't seen all of it, I had to leave and everybody would make fun of me. "There goes Whitey. You'd better start running." When that curfew sounded, we had to be in the house, my brother and I. There I was, almost seventeen years old, I still had to be in the house at nine o'clock when the curfew sounded. It was drilled into us that anybody under sixteen who wasn't off the streets at nine o'clock would be arrested. We really believed in it. I'd run all the way home and get in just as the curfew was sounding. It was the nine o'clock whistle at the fire station and my father would say, "You just about made it this time, kids. Get up to bed."

One time my brother and I had to leave the movies when we were at the Colonial Theater, at five of nine. I said to my brother Bobby that I wasn't going to take this any more. I was going to tell my father that I was fifteen and Bobby was fourteen, but we left a movie that was really exciting and we never saw the end. We were old enough to stay out later.

My brother said, "You tell him. Dad will be sitting there reading the paper and listening to the radio. You tell him." We got into the house and my father said, "You just about made it. Now get up to bed because we're going to get up early to go to the garden with the tools in the car and we're going to weed the gar-

Harold's South End jacket.

den." We scampered upstairs. My brother said, "I thought you were going to say something?" I said, "No, I thought you were."

We didn't dare say anything to Dad. No way. He meant business. I'll tell you, when I came home from the Navy, I was nineteen years old and I still had to be in by ten p.m.

Our group all bought jackets together in 1943 and '44. They were black and silver jackets and they all had South End printed on the back. For thirty cents more you could have your nickname embroidered on the front. For those who couldn't afford it, we'd all chip in twenty-five cents or fifty cents. We all had silver and black jackets and were very proud of that. Later, even the girls bought them. I still have mine. We were the first in the city to have jackets and then, naturally, the Crick Indians purchased jackets, the Christian Shore kids bought special jackets, the North End

The 1944 South End Hawks football team, Harold at top left. The had a 4-1 reecord, losing only to the Rams who would not play them again for the championship.

bunch bought jackets, and finally the Puddle Dock crew.

Portsmouth was still divided amongst its neighborhoods. The Creek Indians were in the western part of the city, and the Christian Shore was directly across the North Mill Pond, up around Dennett Street, Maplewood Avenue and Thornton Street. Then there was the North End, the Italian section, by the railroad tracks—Deer Street, Hanover Street, upper Vaughn Street, the area by the train station. That was really a close-knit group of people. There was the South End and there was Puddle Dock, and we still didn't get along with the Puddle Dockers. We in the South End always had that little hard feeling of animosity. There was a gang-type element in Puddle Dock.

We were a proud section of the city. A lot of outstanding athletes came from the South End. During the outstanding years at the high school with the basketball team, and the football team, half of the players came from the South End.

When I entered high school I was buying my mother a half a pound of pecan roll, every other week, after I collected on my paper route. She loved it and I would bring her home a box—it was about four or five pieces. The people at Fanny Farmer's saw me coming in and out and they asked me one time if I'd like to be a part-time stock boy. They needed somebody to wrap the boxes that customers were ordering for servicemen. I'd have to wrap and label them and take them to the post office. Twice a week, usually a Thursday and a Friday, I'd go into the basement and make up the boxes. They paid me twelve dollars a week. It was a real good part-time job.

The narrow, little store was located right on Congress Street, just west of Vaughan Street. Sometimes I had seven or eight boxes I'd have to take up to the post office and they were filled with assorted candies: hard candy, or with a soft center, or mixed. At Christmas time I had to make two or three trips. That part-time job allowed me to get a job as a packer's helper at twenty cents more an hour at the Portsmouth Naval Shipyard. While everyone else was being hired as a laborer at the age of sixteen, during the summer between their junior and senior years in high school, I was hired as a packer's helper because I had worked in the mailing room at the *Herald* and as the part-time stock boy at Fanny Farmer's candy store.

January—1944

I remember the day my father told me to be sure to go to Peirce Island and take a lunch, stay there half the afternoon after school and I'd see history being made. My father didn't talk too much about the Shipyard because during the war years the old saying "loose lips sink ships" was on everybody's mind. Happenings on the shipyard were very classified.

People who worked for the military, civil defense, or any of the shipyards didn't talk about it, especially the scheduled launchings of the submarines. Even the movement of the troops that were stationed at some of our forts in the seacoast was classified information. We all believed that the enemy was right off our coast.

Nobody knew who would be listening. Posters placed throughout the city warned us that there could be an act of sabotage, or even spies among us.

So my father didn't actually tell us anything—all he said was that history was going to be made at the Shipyard. But we knew it had to be the launching of a sub, maybe a new type of submarine. This was around the end of January of 1944. We found out later the subs USS *Razorback*, the USS *Redfish* and the USS *Ronquil* were the submarines launched that day (three in one day).

My mother had a lunch prepared for us and we got out of school at

Two views of Peirce Island. Harold used to ride his bike across the mounds along the shore. The mounds were the remains of Revolutionary war Fort Washington and were were bulldozed to make way for the city's sewage treatment plant.

one o'clock. I notified the *Herald* I wouldn't be in to work the mailing bench and I had my helper take the paper route. The launching was going to be about two o'clock.

Half the city was there, and my father had tried to keep it such a secret! So we were at the easterly end of Peirce Island, all of us gathered there, and people had their camp chairs and their children and families. We were making like a picnic.

What we found out was that three submarines were going to come down the ways, only we didn't know what time. But we knew high tide was around two o'clock, so it had to be around that time. Sure enough, the whistle blew at the Shipyard—long, steam blasts and the crowd at the Shipyard gathered at dockside roared, and the horns started blowing. And then down came one sub from the ways and a tug took it to dockside. Then another submarine came down the ways, and another, so we saw three subs launched in a period of about three hours.

There was a swimming pool at Peirce Island then but on a much smaller scale then now, and at the easterly end of Peirce Island, there was no treatment plant. It was all wide open. In fact, at the very end were these mounds of loose dirt and old fill that we thought Public Works had dumped. But years later we found out it was Fort Washington, built during the Revolutionary War to protect the harbor from the British. There was nothing left at all except mounds of dirt.

Fort Washington was never manned, but when the treatment plant was built, it was a shame because they bulldozed that over. The only thing that remained was one or two of those mounds of what was Fort Washington, another part of Portsmouth's history lost.

Well, anyway, that was history being made and my father made sure that we saw it because it would be something that we would always remember. It was a big event.

Nothing was reported about any of these subs until after the war was over. If a sub went down and it lost all hands you didn't hear about it until long after the fact. It was never mentioned if it was a Portsmouth-built sub.

The people who worked at the Navy Yard came in and out by bus from Market Square. A bus would take the workers out of the Navy Yard and the coordinator of the bus transportation would yell out, "Wentworth Acres north end! Pannaway Manor straight out!" And people would get on that bus to take them home.

World War II air raid siren atop the Lafayette School.

I was able to see the Shipyard from a window in the attic from my house on South School Street. When we had a blackout you couldn't see any light coming from the Shipyard. Even in our house we had to make sure our curtains were closed. We had to use clothespins on the curtains to make sure that no light got out. As a matter of fact, my father made sure that none of our lamps, a table lamp or a floor lamp, was ever near a window.

On our cars we had to paint the top half of the headlights—all the cars in the city were compelled by the Department of Motor Vehicles in Concord to paint half the headlights black. The point was if the enemy was flying over they wouldn't see anything. They couldn't detect the city, or especially the Shipyard.

We'd have an air raid drill once a month. The newspapers would have a small article to tell us when it was going to be. It was usually about three or four o'clock in the afternoon. This was after the children were home from school, after things had quieted down.

When the air raid sounded, a horn went off at all the schools in the city. They had a big canister that looked like a bird feeder and that was they siren. When it sounded you could hear it everywhere. There was no doubt about it. The schools that had a siren on top of them were: Haven, Sherburne, Franklin, Wentworth, Atlantic Heights, Whipple School, and the Farragut. The Farragut School, off Vaughan Street on School Street, was the second oldest school in the city. It was demolished during the urban renewal of the early 1960s. That was one of the biggest losses the city has ever had, a beautiful building. The Haven School was the oldest.

I was there when the city demolished the Farragut School. They

The Farragut school was located on School Street.

came in with a two-and-a-half-ton ball, but they couldn't really swing the ball because the street was narrow. The ball bounced off the building like it was nothing. It didn't even crack the walls. Then they had to move the crane out and they came in with a big bucket crane and they had to peck away at the roof. They had to be careful because there were houses right up close to it. The school took care of all the Italian and other families in the North End. It was a beautiful, three-story brick building.

When I was fifteen, I was still in the Boy Scouts. I got eighteen merit badges and my mother was anxious for me to make Eagle; you need-ed twenty-one merit badges to make Eagle. I'd been appointed a patrol leader and was also selected as an assistant air raid warden.

That meant when the siren went off, and I was out of school, I'd have to patrol along South Street from where Newcastle Avenue and South Street meet, and down to the corner of South Mill Street. I'd walk back and forth. I'll never forget the time a police patrol car went by and the police-

man rolled down his window and yelled out: "Hey, kid, get off the street."
I showed him my armband, which had a red cross on it, my helmet, and
my nightstick and said, "I'm an assistant air raid warden." He said, "Oh,
I'm sorry kid. Sorry kid."

My route was the directive of the air raid warden who lived across
the street from me; his name was Harry Wendell, who owned Wendell's
Hardware store downtown in Market Square. I had to make sure all the
houses were blacked out and everyone was off the street. That was most
important. The warning came maybe between three and six o'clock and
everybody scattered. Everybody went in and pulled their shades. You
never saw any activity whatsoever. There were air raid wardens and assis-
tants posted all throughout the city.

We had an air raid maybe once a month and each one lasted about
fifteen or twenty minutes. The air raids started in 1942, not long after Pearl
Harbor, which of course was on Dec. 7, 1941.

As the war was winding down and the Marines started to advance
in the Pacific and take islands, and as we were getting control of the
Western Front, as the Germans were being defeated, and people were
being liberated in different parts of Europe, the air raids and the drills
started to dwindle down.

1943—Limited Supply

I want to talk about rationing. Once a month my mother would take me
down and we'd have to sign up for rationing and get our ration stamps.
That office was located in a little place down on Fleet Street, between
Congress and Hanover, and we went in and had our name checked off and
we were given a book with a certain number of rationing stamps. The
office was run by the county in a garage showroom.

It was very important to use these stamps when we bought coffee,
or any kind of meat—if they had meat. Usually we only found baloney or
hot dogs, maybe sometimes hamburger. If we ever found steak or chops in
the showcase—that was very rare. Both coffee and meat were very scarce
and there was also rationing for butter, cheese, and gasoline.

My mother would buy a slab of baloney and slice it very thin. We
always had baloney sandwiches. My mother made a lot of stews. She
knew how to make things out of practically nothing. A big deal was fried
bread on a Sunday night. She'd mix the dough with yeast and then cover
it on the back of the stove and it would rise up during the night and then

The battleship USS Texas *visited Portsmouth in 1939.*

she'd fry it. That was called fried dough. It was small, like a muffin. But we never had real butter; it was always margarine. I hated that imitation butter.

When we bought something, we paid with cash and then we also had to give over a stamp. In the showcase there would be a sign that said, "Hamburger, twelve cents a pound and three ration stamps."

A lot of everyday items were in short supply during the war. Women couldn't even buy a pair of nylons. Anybody who could get a brand new pair of nylons—that was like getting gold. They were using the nylon fabric for parachutes. Everything that was rationed was being used in the military.

The food was going into K rations for the hundreds of thousands of soldiers who were all over the world. The gasoline was going to the military vehicles. There was a reason behind all the rationing. Americans never questioned the sacrifice, and were very patriotic. Once, every elementary school was asked to have an aluminum pot-and-pan drive, with two months to collect as many pots and pans as they could. The elementary school that collected the most would be given a prize. We boys would be knocking on doors. We would go to the town dump off Jones Avenue and rake over the dump to find the old pots and pans. We found, over a two-month period, enough pots and pans to reach the second story of the

Haven School in one pile. A picture was taken in front of the elementary school with kids the who had received the award.

The aluminum was taken away and melted down to be used for armament—but everything was collected: copper, brass, aluminum, and tires. Most people had to use retreads. You couldn't buy a new tire during the war years.

One of our biggest thrills was finding out how the war was going. We'd listen to the nine o'clock news on the radio, Gabriel Heatter and Walter Winchell. There were certain news commentators that we had an interest in listening to. They all had their own little niche. The war, of course, in 1944, was going well for us and it looked like the end was almost near.

Portsmouth was a center of activity; we weren't on the sidelines. The old diesel fleet subs were really the backbone of the war effort. We were fascinated by the returning Marines, the sailors, and the Army personnel who had gone into the service early, maybe at the age of sixteen or seventeen, and were returning to tell us what had happened. We'd meet a friend in uniform and he'd tell us where he'd been and what he'd done— very exciting to us younger kids.

They'd bring us back a souvenir. We had one teacher, whose name was Frances Malloy, and he taught drafting. He was a collector of daggers and swords and mementos. Before the war was over, he had a valuable collection of swords, daggers, knives and machetes from all over the world. Who knows where they ended up? He lived into his nineties and was one of my favorite high school teachers. You never heard anybody speak out against the war—never, never, never.

We'd hang out downtown wearing our South End jackets. On a Friday or Saturday night we'd be in front of the Jarvis's, which was located right in Market Square. We'd be talking and hanging out just as the kids do today in front of North Church. We'd talk about school, the war, the girls, and the movies. We'd talk about anything. There was always someone who was a little bit older whose father would let him bring a car downtown. We didn't have any gas to go anywhere, but we'd all crowd in that car—six or seven of us in that car—and we'd sit there and talk. The windows would get all steamed up. Nobody had any money or ration stamps, but the father would let the son who was sixteen or seventeen take the car. He was a big deal.

1944 comes to a close

As I mentioned earlier, my father was starting to make a little money, and we had a few things, but in our house we still didn't have a bathroom. I remember in the latter part of 1944 we had the landlord come down for about the third time to see where he could put in a bathroom for us. My father and mother just got tired of the tub in the middle of the kitchen floor on a Sunday night with the papers down on the floor, the doors shut and heating water on the stove. The toilet was still in the cellar. The landlord promised that he would put a bathroom in on the second floor, and he designated a space for where it would go, but it never happened. That's why my mother and father started to look around for a house, finally, in the middle of 1946. That's when they found a house to buy. So we had been there in that house for ten years without a bathtub. That would be a good name for this book, "Ten years without a bathroom."

The holidays were still exciting. We went places, did things; we got some clothes and we started having a few more presents under the Christmas tree. We always had a live Christmas tree.

The war was coming to an end now. The Marines were island hopping in the Pacific. The war was going well in Europe. The boys were coming home and we're meeting them. We admired them for doing their patriotic duty for the country.

1945

The first thing that took place in 1945 that was quite devastating was the death of Franklin Delano Roosevelt. My father and mother admired him. They made us gather around the radio and listen to all the broadcasts in reference to his death. My father was a strong Democrat, but he never really talked politics with me. Roosevelt was the originator of the New Deal and the CCC camps and the WPA, the PWA. He brought jobs to the country. And my father and mother thought that he was the most effective president we ever had. They were devastated when he passed away so suddenly.

He had brought people through the Depression and the war. But even up until the end I never realized that he had polio. Even when I was fourteen or fifteen years old, I always thought he just sat down in these open air cars, or whenever he was in the back of a train, just sitting, that that was his ordinary way of just greeting the people. We had seen him downtown in 1939, as I said before. I can't remember any public demonstration about FDR's death in Portsmouth. It was very quiet.

As time went on we knew the next president would be Harry S.

Truman, but there were a lot of questions. What will he do? How will the war go? How will it end or will things continue the way they've been going with our allies? That was the most important thing. People were curious, that's all. People just didn't know what was going to happen. There was excitement about some of the statements Truman had made—his hard-nosed approach to issues—and some of the language he used, and that got people's attention.

The Portsmouth Naval Shipyard

I turned sixteen in July and at the post office I saw a notice that, for the summer, they were going to hire fifty laborers at the Shipyard. Once we saw the notice and what the pay was going to be, we all went down to the office. All us South Enders went together, and got the papers to be a laborer.

I filled out my paperwork to say that I worked at the mailing room at the *Portsmouth Herald* and as a part-time stock boy at the Fannie Farmer's. So when my paperwork came back I was hired at fifteen cents more an hour as a packer's helper. I got my paper's about ten days after I had turned sixteen. I went over there and took my physical and got my badge and started working just right after that, about two weeks after my birthday. I got my badge and was showing it off, because I was a packer's helper, and all my friends were going on as laborers.

I was quite proud of working on the yard. My mother cut me down a pair of my father's old overalls, and I had an old lunchbox that my father wasn't using, an old black lunch box, with a thermos bottle in it. And I took the bus in front of my house on South School Street, but I would always walk home because I wanted to make sure that everyone playing basketball in the Haven School grounds saw me with my lunch box and my badge.

There were many people in the room I worked in. I was located on the fifth floor of the supply department in Building 153. I was helping them pack the electronics that came from General Electric: switches, light fixtures, and transformers. All those items that were made at GE in Somersworth were packed in big wooden crates with excelsior and shipped out to other shipyards where they were building surface ships for the war effort.

The crates had to be packed just so to prevent damage, were stenciled, and wired with a wire band. There was a packer who taught me the proper way to do it. These were huge, huge crates. I liked the job, I liked the money, and I liked the men I worked with, but the general foreman talked me out of staying.

The job was for sixty-five to ninety days and that was it. I forget what the pay was, something like $1.75 an hour. It was not bad, good money for a forty-hour week. My first full paycheck was a nice surprise. Then I could buy a few things for myself and start a bank account. I put my money into the old First National Bank downtown, right on Pleasant Street. I wanted a car, was sixteen years old, and I wanted to get a car someday and get my license.

I worked all summer long and I almost didn't go back to school. One day the general foreman of the supply department called me into his office, and I was kind of frightened. I didn't know what I could have done. He shut the door and said, "Harold, I understand you might not go back to school and stay over here on the job?" And I said, "Yes, sir, I certainly would. It's a wonderful job."

"Let me tell you something," he said—I think his last name was Smiley—"You get your diploma," he said. "You finish out your senior year. Then you come back over to the Shipyard and come under the apprentice program. That's the smart way to go."

Now, nobody had ever talked to me like that before. My mother and father—neither one of them had finished high school—so they didn't think high school was important. They knew I wasn't going to be going to college, there was no money for college, and I wasn't taking the preparatory college course. I was taking the mechanical arts course, but this gentleman took the time to explain how important an education was. I'll never forget that. It kind of turned my life around, that little incident of talking to me and convincing me not to stay at the Shipyard. So I went back to school.

When the time came I had to give my notice and I went back to school. I think I had two days off that whole summer of 1945.

But before we get back to school I want to talk about August 1945. That was when the atomic bombs were dropped on Nagasaki and Hiroshima. There were two atomic bomb explosions, one on August 6th and one on August 9th, three days apart. Nobody knew it was going to happen, nobody even knew a bomb was being tested.

Two or three days after that, pictures started appearing in newspapers and more information about the thousands that had been killed was made public. We kids could not believe that one bomb could do that much damage; we didn't realize what the atomic bomb was. We talked about it, we read about it. Later, in our science class at school, the teacher explained how atomic energy worked and how it is produced.

As time went on and we read about it, we realized how devastating the bombing was, how thousands of people were killed, and then we realized how serious radiation is. We hadn't known it could affect you in years to come. But in terms of the war, we thought it would shorten the war, but we didn't think it would shorten it that fast. In fact, V-J Day also came about in August of 1945. That was when the Japanese surrendered and it was September 2nd when the peace treaty was signed in Tokyo Bay aboard the USS *Missouri*. It was just two years later in September of 1947 in the Navy that I would be stationed on the battleship USS *Missouri*, BB-63.

On V-J Day in 1945, however, I wasn't allowed to go downtown. But we could hear the noise and the people yelling and screaming and the horns and the bells. Every church bell in the city was ringing and the whistle on the Shipyard went off. It was a whistle that functioned by steam so it couldn't go off but every thirty or forty-five minutes or so because they had to build up the steam pressure. There was laughter, and a parade downtown. I asked my mother to please let me go down—they were actually broadcasting from WHEB on the scene—and it was really something. But I wasn't allowed to leave the Haven School yard. So all of us kids on the South End marched around with our whistles on the school grounds making some noise. That was the extent of celebrating our V-J Day.

My mother wouldn't let us go downtown because there would be so much drinking; all the servicemen would be out on the street. No way— the mothers in the South End kept their children pretty secure and close to home because of the rowdiness. We had our own little party talking and hollering and whistling. Someone had a portable radio going, and we turned it up as loud as we could and put it on the wooden picnic table out in the school grounds—that was it.

But a few days later, some of us walked up Pleasant Street—we always walked in groups of six or eight or ten, four in front, three in back, always talking—and we went through the town and you could tell there had been a party. There were beer bottles all over the place; there were all kinds of stuff. You could tell something had happened. V-J Day was the only time Portsmouth had an organized parade without a permit. People just organized it themselves. The storefronts closed up and people came out onto the street and they started a parade in a very short time.

But I want to back up a little bit. Four of us went down to the recruitment office on the first of June, before the atomic bomb dropped. They had a promotion for recruiting: If you joined with four friends they guaranteed you would stay with those four friends after boot camp or basic training. So the four of us went down, but they took only one. He was big for his age and he lied a little bit. You were supposed to be seventeen years old with a mother's permission. When I tell my two children that today they can't believe that I tried to get in the military at the age of sixteen. But I only weighed about ninety-six or ninety-seven pounds and so I was refused and told to go home and put on some weight. This was the Navy I was trying to get into. They had a recruiting office at what now is called the Connie Bean Center. Then it was the Army and Navy Center.

I took my father's long coat and I had a soft hat on. I stood on my tiptoes. I was trying to act older, but it didn't work. They took that one guy, though, and he went into the Navy and he saw a little bit of action—not too much. But we all wanted to become part of the patriotic group that the South End was known for. We admired the servicemen we knew from our section of the city so much.

Another incident in the latter part of September was the day my father told me to go over to Peirce Island. There was a U-Boat, my father said, that had surrendered off the coast of Massachusetts. My father said the Coast Guard was bringing it into the Portsmouth Naval Shipyard under escort at a certain time on Saturday. "But don't tell anybody," he said again. I went over there and, sure enough, the whole city was there again to see the same thing. This was the second time this had happened to me with my father telling me to keep a secret like that. But he said it was history being made again. "There's a German U-Boat coming in and you get over there early, get a good place out on the point." I had my old-fashioned field glasses with me when the sub came up the Piscataqua under Coast Guard escort.

The Germans were all standing topside, all in dress uniforms; they were still a very proud Navy. When they docked the boat the sailors gave a salute. They didn't have the German flag flying—there was no flag at all. But they still saluted as they left the boat going off the gangway. We stayed there half the day, watching them unloading stores, and seeing the little ceremonies that took place, and then they took the prisoners to the naval prison by bus.

We couldn't believe we were seeing the enemy. It was exciting, I'm telling you. We didn't really know what they were going to look like, but looking through the field glasses they looked like they were a sharp Navy, but glad the war was over. Now some people say that a U-Boat came up into Portsmouth harbor and got in through the nets and surfaced near the naval prison, right off the Shipyard, but I don't believe that. There are stories, but I think it's a little bit of a myth.

The Shipyard was still going strong even though the war was winding down. They still had boats on the ways and in dry dock. But they did slow down a little bit; there was no more overtime, there was no more twelve-fourteen hour days, seven days a week. The layoffs didn't really start until the 1950s.

But I was without a job. So I went down to the *Herald* and talked to the foreman in the press department. They had lost two men to the draft and they were short-handed. Bill Caldwell was the foreman of the press department. He kind of liked me, and he knew me from all my years of doing the paper route and working in the mailing room. He had two daughters and he didn't have any sons, so he kind of took a liking to me as a son. He wanted to know what time I got out of school and I said I got out at one o'clock. He said, "Could you be here at quarter after one?" and I said the school was right around the corner. "If I run down Porter Street I can be at the back of the mechanical shop where the press is in a matter of ten minutes." So he said, "All right. How would you like to work in the press department? We'll teach you, but you have to work every day part-time and all day Saturday." There was a press run at one o'clock Saturday. I said, "Sure, love to." So they hired me and I worked every afternoon from quarter after one—the press run was 2:05, that was important—and by a little after three—I was out of there.

I had plenty of time to go home and do my homework and do the chores around the house. It was a nice little job. I was learning to ink up, make stereotype plates, and set up tension on the press during the press run. My job was to make sure the huge rolls of newsprint didn't get carried away as they rotated. We created tension around wooden blocks at the end of the shaft. If the rolls started carrying away and revolving faster then the newspaper was going up through the web and down through the fly, then we'd in trouble. Each roll had to have a different tension on the end of the shaft, onto the blocks. That was an interesting job. I learned that pretty fast. I never did learn how to work the buttons on the press. That was the foreman's job. I worked there from the latter part of September in 1945 to June of 1946, all during my senior year in high school.

At that time, the rationing and the air raids, everything started to wind down. Rationing did continue for a short time, but naturally there were no more air raid drills. We still had a shortage of gasoline, and the women still had no silk stockings. We noticed a little more food in the corner grocery store, a little more meat, a little more coffee, sugar, and flour. The servicemen were all coming back.

In November 1945 I told my mother that in scouting I had earned all my merit badges. I had been appointed junior assistant patrol leader and I was going to make Eagle in February. My mother was quite proud of that. She told everybody in the neighborhood. When the second week of February came in 1946, we went up to the North Church Parish House, which is now the Salvation Army home, on Middle Street. That's where four of us who made Eagle in the city of Portsmouth received our awards. There was a court of awards presentation, and the Daniel Webster Council executives came down from Manchester and Concord to present the awards to us. All the families and the relatives were there. The place was crowded. There were 100, 150 people.

It started snowing—I'll never forget this—the night before the ceremony and it snowed all day. We went into the hall about five or six in the afternoon and were barely able to get there because of the snowdrifts. When we came out at eleven o'clock, my mother and I didn't think we were going to make it home. My brother had stayed home to take care of the children. My father was working another shift that night, so he wasn't able to go. But it was a terrible, terrible northeaster. My mother had never learned to drive so we had walked everywhere.

My father had tried to teach her once. He came back after taking her in the car out to a side road in Stratham one Sunday. I was only about fourteen years old. He came back in the afternoon, came in and didn't say a word, didn't talk to anybody. But he called me over later and said, "Junior, do you know you've got just about the slowest mother in the world?" "What do you mean Dad?" I said. He started telling me how he was trying to teach her to drive on a dirt road where there was no traffic and they ended up in a ditch—right off the road and into a ditch—had to have a farmer with a tractor pull them out.

My father was furious and never tried to teach her again. There was no driver's education, nothing like that back in those days. There was no instruction. People had to learn on their own to get a permit. You read the book, you watched your father, and he took you out and tried to help. He let you know when you were ready.

At the end of the year, 1945, the war was over and a lot of military friends were coming back to spend Christmas with their fathers and mothers and their families. It was kind of a touchy situation because we didn't know whether to go down and knock on the doors and greet our friends or just wait to see them, either walking on the streets or downtown. Maybe we'd see them having a hot chocolate or a Coke downtown at one of the soda fountains.

We didn't know whether they wanted to be by themselves. So we used to go down and hang around in front of their homes waiting for them to come out. We'd greet them and shake their hands and have a picture taken. They were still in uniform and they loved to tell us about where they had been and what they'd done—particularly the Marines. These Marines were only nineteen- or twenty-year old kids who saw action in the South Pacific and they told us about their ribbons. They explained everything about these ribbons, how they were earned, the campaigns, and the stars—what they meant to them. It was very impressive to us kids.

Returning servicemen were very open with us, they were glad to see us. But in order to talk about the war, we had to get them off to one side, away from their mothers and fathers. Not many of them were married. They were only kids themselves, just a few years older than we were. We really admired them because they were patriots. We had grown up with them, played with them, gone to school with them, and all of a sudden they got drafted, or they volunteered to go, and then they were gone.

There was also the recognition that Portsmouth had lost her fair share of kids. I know of two from the South End, who were killed, who were in Marine landings in the South Pacific. We were glad that World War II was over. In fact, at Christmas time my father and mother made us all get dressed up and we went to a special Christmas Eve service at the Christ Church, to thanking God for the war being over and the boys returning. I'll never forget that.

Chapter Four: Military Service

1946

This was a good year. I started showing a little more improvement academically because I had more time to study since I only had the one job and I was home by 3:30. It was getting a little bit crowded at home. We were growing up. My father still had his own room because all during the war it was important for him to get a good night's sleep and not be disturbed. My brother and I were still up in the attic, and the two sisters were in another room on the other side of the attic.

Girls are coming into the picture. We were starting to go down to the Wentworth Hotel when we knew the girls were getting off work. They were waitresses, housekeeping people, and the ones who were tending bar—these were all girls who were attending college. They were respected and well trained and they came back every year. The Wentworth hired nothing but the best.

We knew it was a good place to meet a girl and get a date. The hotel had a dormitory down in the back—we weren't allowed in the front part of the Wentworth. In fact one time I went up to the ballroom and I was told to go back to my room, sir, and put my tie on. In other words, that was a polite way of saying: "You're out of here kid." I had to be home early, anyway.

1946—Eighteen in July

There wasn't much celebrating on New Year's Eve. We all gathered around the radio and mother might make something special like deep-fried bread or a big bag of popcorn, maybe with a lot of butter on it. We'd make popcorn balls. But there was never anything special for the New Year's celebration.

Early in 1946, I joined the YMCA, which was 141 Congress Street, over Goodman's Clothing Store. I joined the Y—it didn't cost much, something like fifteen or eighteen dollars a year. They had a shower and locker facilities where I took my Saturday afternoon shower. It eliminated the whole bathtub routine in the middle of the kitchen floor on a Saturday night. That was a load off my shoulders. I'd play a little basketball, work up a little sweat, and then have an excuse to go downstairs to take a shower. My mother liked that idea.

I was high school senior, and learned that if I blended in with the right crowd I could get involved in sports. I was too small for basketball or football, so I thought I'd go out for track. I was about 5-foot-2, not very tall. I weighted about ninety-five, pounds, very thin. I was wiry and fast, so Coach Culbberson allowed me to train for the mile. I never finished up front. If there were ten or fifteen in the pack I'd finish sixth or seventh. I tried to get a letter, but I never did receive a letter or a sweater—never did receive my 'P' from Portsmouth High.

The coach and my friends on the track team worked with me. I tried different things—the 440 and the 880—but the mile was the one I could finish even though I was never up there really competing. Nashua was our big rival. Nashua and Manchester had the best track teams. And Dover had a good track team at that time. We'd get on the bus and go from school to school to compete.

In the summer I worked full time at the *Herald*. I was up at 7:30, taking my lunch pail, and they taught me to become a pressman. The press was a Goss, a 4-unit letterpress, web-type—printing a maximum of sixteen pages when it was fully running. First I was in charge of the tension, down in the basement when the press is running. Next they moved me upstairs onto the first floor because I was small and thin and could get in between the units when the press was running to work the keys in the ink wells. There were four units and I was in a charge of two. I would take the paper off the fly and look at it to catch the highlight—one column would be dark, another light.

Each column of the newspaper had to be regulated with a key in the ink well, which would allow more or less ink to go to each column. I'd look at the sheet of eight columns and maybe see two columns that were kind of light and would reach down and open up the keys to allow more ink into the column. So I was being trained for that and I liked that pretty well. Later I was put in the stereotype department where I transferred the plates from the raised type onto a mat that was put into a circular casting box. I pumped molten lead into the top of the casting, then cut the casting

Portsmouth Herald *Back shop printers and pressmen taking a break on Porter Street.*

tail and head off, and that casting cylinder would go onto the press. This was a very skilled trade at that time.

I had a full-time job and I was doing everything in the stereotype department except running the press. I loved working at the newspaper. It was exciting when the press was wide open and the ink mist was in the air with the smell of paper dust and the papers were coming out the fly. It was exciting, especially when the publisher came out of the newsroom waving a bulletin that came off the Teletype, "Stop the presses! Open page one! Bulletin! Whitehouse, get up here. Get this set up on the Linotype machine. We want to get this out onto the street as an extra!" A bulletin that broke halfway through the run—they don't do that today.

Most of my friends were working downtown in neighborhood stores, at the corner grocery stores or at apparel shops, or boutiques. Some were working as laborers since there was some construction going on. Guys were hot topping, digging ditches—run-of-the-mill laborer work. The guys who had come back from the military were trying to find jobs, but the jobs were scarce and they didn't want to do mediocre laborer-type work or work in a grocery store where they were only paid fifty or sixty cents an hour. They wanted to find a real job or use the GI Bill for schooling. An employer was compelled to take an employee back if he had been drafted.

The South End continued to change. A few houses were being painted because the landlords would furnish paint. We went down to see our
landlord, F.A. Gray, to get some wallpaper. My mother knew how to wallpaper, but we had to strip the paper off the wall first. I'll never forget that.
My mother and I took a hot-water sponge and stripped the wallpaper off
and what a mess we made. We got the plaster all wet and started digging
it out with a putty knife. We gouged out the plaster and had to re-plaster
all those holes, and then we had to dry it out. We made a terrible mess.

There were no steamers in those days, so we couldn't rent one, but
we stripped all the wallpaper off in that little living room—it was only ten
feet by twelve feet—and then we wallpapered that room. We put a border
on and everything. We worked off an ironing board, with paste mixed up
in a bucket and a wide brush. My mother knew how to fold the wallpaper
as it was being pasted up. She'd get up on a little ladder and hang it and
line up the pattern with each piece she put up. It really looked good afterwards. But preparing it was a pain.

And then in the summer the landlord gave us paint. The other people in the back half of the house didn't want to be bothered, so we only
painted our half of the house. But everybody was doing this. The landlords were allowing the renters to update their homes to make them look
a little better. The people who owned their homes were also painting, putting new steps in, and making their homes a little more presentable. Many
houses were old with broken windows, or boarded up. People had been
living hand to mouth and didn't care too much how the property looked.

There was still a lot of work at the Navy Yard; they hadn't started
cutting back just yet. There were still boats on the building ways and submarines in the dry-docks that had to be completed to get back into the
fleet; the war had ended so abruptly. If somebody retired they wouldn't
replace him. People left on their own, went back from where they came
from, back to the Brooklyn Navy Yard, the Philadelphia Naval Shipyard,
and the Boston Yard.

I was still friends with the kids I knew when I was younger, still
hanging around together, still making model airplanes. Ralphie, Donald,
Herbie, Arthur—we were all friends. Nobody had a car, but Ralphie's
father let him take a 1937 Ford once in a while. We'd go downtown and sit
in the car, or go to the Demolay together, or have a soda at one of the corner soda fountains. I still had to be home by nine and the shift changed at
the Wentworth around nine p.m. so there wasn't a lot of time to meet girls.

Market Square, circa 1950, where Harold and his friends used to hang out.

The only time I was allowed to stay and see a complete movie was when my father was on the afternoon shift. He'd go in at three and he wouldn't be home until eleven at night. So on those days my mother would say I want you home right after the movies. She'd have a schedule and knew when one movie ended and another started. I'd have to be home five minutes after that movie ended. There was a little leeway there, even though I was seventeen years old. She was just trying to keep me from getting into trouble.

I didn't tell you how I lost my bicycle. It was over at Peirce Island, and I had to go to my best friend George, who was king of the Puddle Dock gang, and ask him where my bike was. "I'll get back to you in a couple of days, Whitey," he said. We were only in the fifth or sixth grade. Sure enough, he found my bike. Someone had taken it and thrown it into the bushes on the easterly end of Peirce Island.

You never laid anything down. Your baseball glove was kept on your belt. If you laid a bat down you watched it all the time. Things had feet—I'm telling you—they would walk. People would steal baseballs—

Harold, left and his friends Ann, Paul, and cousin Donald acting up before the boys left for basic training. The boys were only seventeen and too young for alcohol, so the "bar" was just a set for photos.

you always put your name on a baseball in ink. If you had a wood-burning set, you'd burn your name into your baseball bat and just about everything you owned.

My mother wouldn't let me take my bike over to Peirce Island very often. You'd walk over because if you laid it down and you didn't lock it with a chain, the thing would be missing.

It was a nice warm summer. I made about forty dollars a week at the *Herald*. I had a bank account, saved some money, bought some clothes, and gave my mother a little extra to help out at the house. I was seventeen years old and thinking about the Navy. I didn't tell my mother, I didn't say anything until April or May of 1946. The reason I wanted to go into the Navy was because you could go in for a two-year enlistment. They were trying to build it up, and you could go in on the buddy program, and we could stay together; that's what we tried to do before. But then it was a four-year enlistment. After the war they reduced it to a two-year enlistment and you came in under the GI Bill if you enlisted before December 1946. You got college, a bonus, and classified as a World War II veteran, with all the benefits of the GI Bill.

My mother didn't like the idea at first, but then I explained the benefits that I would be getting. I didn't have any money for college, but mother had five other children to think about educating, especially my sister Barbara, who was brilliant in school, the fifth child down, and the only one who did go to college.

My mother would have to sign for me to go into the Navy because I was only seventeen years old and she agreed to do it. I graduated the third week in June and, in the fourth week, June 24th, I was sworn into the Navy in Manchester, New Hampshire.

I had gone down to the recruiting office in the community center on Daniel Street with Dick, Dave, and Alvin. We were all going to be stationed together, either aboard ship or at a naval station. We took the oath and the agreement was we'd be picked up on June 24, 1946, at seven o'clock in the morning. Sure enough, there came the recruiter with his car. I had a little duffle bag, with a few clothes, that's it. Before I left my mother hugged me and it was the first time I had ever seen tears in her eyes.

I was finally leaving home. I was the helper, the oldest. I was responsible. I promised her I'd send her my allotment, so she could take care of the other children, all the time I was in the Navy.

I was kind of anxious to see what this was going to be like. I knew I was going to go to the Bainbridge Naval Training Center outside Baltimore, and it was in the middle of the summer. That was what I was worried about—the heat. It was the worst time to join the Navy. But I wanted to get in under the GI Bill, I didn't want to wait any longer, so we got sworn in and bused down to Baltimore the next day. We had to stay at the YMCA in Manchester the night before. The bus to Baltimore was filled with forty or more men from all over the state. We didn't think about the war flaring up again.

1946 June ——-Bainbridge, Maryland

Bainbridge was a routine boot camp situation. A ditty bag was issued, and a set of clothes. We got a haircut with a minor physical at the end of the day. We got a bunk number with also a company that we were assigned to. Next we met our training officer who was in charge of us for the next eight weeks. There was classroom schooling and work detail, plus rifle training. We learned how to stand watches, fight fires aboard ship, properly identify aircraft and naval ships, practical instruction on naval customs, and some training on first aid, water safety, and survival aboard ship. Every day a certain amount of time was dedicated to physical fitness. After the eight weeks of training, we were either assigned to further schooling or sea duty.

At boot camp we became a Rooster company very quickly. That meant that our company was outstanding and was reviewed by a group of officers. We carried a special flag that identified our company as outstanding. It meant that we were first in line to eat, first privileges for the commissary, and special barracks duty.

If our company showed extraordinary performance in marching with our platoon leader, then special honors were given. We held all our drills on an open field known as the grinder. It was an area of sand and dirt. The dust was unbelievable and very hot, especially during the month of July.

Unfortunately, I came down with pneumonia. First I had cold. I didn't take care of it and I turned myself into sickbay with a temperature of 102. So I was taken from my company, spent ten days in the hospital, and then released back into a different company. I lost all my friends that I joined the Navy with back in Portsmouth. They were advancing and I was two weeks behind in my training.

I did fine at boot camp because it wasn't much different from when I was growing up. I had a curfew at home and I had one in the Navy. There was a regulation of dress at home and in the Navy. There was eating at a certain time in both places. The only difference was living in a barracks with eighty men. But the lights still went out at nine p.m. It was no different for me. I didn't complain—I fell right in line.

This was a period when any one of the military—a soldier, a sailor, a Marine—was very well respected. We hitchhiked everywhere—never got on a bus or a train. We had no problem hitchhiking home from Norfolk, Virginia, or Philadelphia and getting three or four rides all the way up to Boston. Through the South or the Midwest or anywhere throughout the country, you could hitchhike. Even the attendant at a tollbooth would try to get you a ride with a long-haul trucker. They'd stop these truckers and ask, "Where are you going?"

"I'm going to Tucson."

"Hey, I got a sailor right here that's headed for San Francisco."

That's how it was—I did hitchhike across country when I first got discharged. That was in 1948 when I had thirty days leave and went to California.

After eight weeks, I graduated from boot camp and came home. I

The Whitehouse family bought their new home at 173 Madison street.

got a ten-day leave before I had to report for duty. My duty station was to pick up a heavy cruiser, the *Macon* (CA 132), at Philadelphia Naval Shipyard at a certain date. I came home in the middle of September 1946. I got off the bus at Market Square with my duffle bag, and dress whites on and started walking home. When I got close to my home, I cut across the playground and noticed that the house where I had been living for the past ten years looked vacant! I looked into the windows, and there was nobody there. I knocked on the door of the other half of the house, and asked, "Where's my mother and father and family?"

"Don't you know?" they said, "They moved last week! They moved up to the west end of the city—up on Madison Street."

I didn't know because of the mail situation. When you're in the Navy you get a lot of mail at once—it could be four or five days of mail. My mother had written to me saying the rent had gone up from $18 to $20 a month and my father had said, "We're out of here." And he had looked at a house on Madison Street. He had cashed in some of his war bonds and bought if for $2,500. It was a big, old-fashioned two-story colonial.

Seaman Harold, standing at right, and a buddy; and the USS Macon *(CA132).*

My old neighbors took me in their car up to Madison Street. Here I was finally out of the South End, but not living at home any more. My mother was proud of the house they bought. She showed me the new white refrigerator she had never had before, a new gas stove, and a hot air heating system fired by coal. Every room in the house was heated now—no more cold up stairs in the bedroom.

But the most important thing was that they had a bathroom. This bathroom had a tub with legs and a sink and hopper all in one room, and everybody was happy as a lark. My mother and father and the children were so proud of this new home. I stayed home for ten days, and then I reported to Philadelphia Naval Shipyard to board the *Macon*.

In the Navy, I teamed up with some buddies from another company who were from Rochester, Farmington, and Milton. They told me that if I came home on a Saturday night there was a dance called the Rendezvous in downtown Rochester, up over a drugstore. They had a live band and there were a lot of girls. So no sooner did I get home, I put my whites on. My mother said I looked sharp. I didn't have a car and so I took a bus for ten cents into Dover and then took a transfer from Dover into Rochester—fifteen cents.

I met my friends who were also in uniform. The girls were on one side and the boys on the other. When the band started up on stage and everybody mingled in the middle. There was one girl, sitting all by herself who wasn't taken. I was kind of bashful still. I hadn't been able to get to meet too many girls, but started to dance with this one girl. I found out we had similar families because she came from a family of ten, three brothers and five sisters, and her parents—so we had a lot in common. And she was also the oldest and she had a lot of responsibility. She was still in her senior year at Spaulding High School, and I liked her right away. Her name was Ruth Kent. All of the girls her age went to the dances. There were not too many servicemen, that's why these guys told me to go up to the Rendezvous. So I danced with Ruth until midnight. And then I didn't see her for quite a while afterwards.

I went to Philadelphia and got aboard my ship, the USS *Macon*. We stayed in port in Philadelphia for another two weeks, with no leave except for short weekend passes. I saw Philadelphia for the first time.

In all the foreign ports and cities I would take a tour. I'd team up with a person whose interest was the same as mine and we'd get to see what the city had to offer from a historical nature; we'd find a guide. That's what I was interested in, I don't know why. I was always interested in the historic value of Portsmouth, too.

We left Philadelphia about the last part of September in 1946. We were told we'd be at sea in the Caribbean maneuvering, and making ports of call, for the next six months. And that's what we did. We went to Kingston, Jamaica, Guantanamo Bay in Cuba, and two or three other ports in the Caribbean. The most important thing I remember is that we anchored out in Guantanamo. There wasn't much there in terms of the naval station; a small beer garden and a commissary and some gift shops—that's all there was. You took the motor launch in—the ship was too large to tie up to a pier. I can only imagine what's there now.

We went into Havana, imagine that? That's when Batista was the dictator. We were able to get into Havana by train. We had 1600 liberty and had to be back by 0-1200, which is midnight. It was an hour's ride by train and an hour back, so we didn't have much time to view the city.

Havana to me was very primitive, real ghetto-type living. There wasn't anything modern and we saw very few cars—mostly just donkey carts. The housing made out of scrap metal or scrap wood. It was kind of depressing, it really was. We were told to never travel alone and never go off the main drag. We traveled in groups of four or five, we'd buy gifts, watch the people, sit in the parks, and walked around to the waterfront.

Our main military mission was mostly goodwill. After World War II, large U. S. ships would pull into foreign ports as a goodwill gesture. People would line up by the hundreds to come aboard the ship.

We came back to Philadelphia right after the New Year, 1947, and I went home for leave. I didn't go to Rochester because my brother had just turned seventeen in December and he was talking about quitting school and joining the Navy. There he was in his junior year and he was going to quit. I told him not to do it, but it wasn't long after that my mother wrote to me—she used to write me every other day—and sure enough, Bobby had come home with an application for my mother to sign and so he was in the Navy. His boot training was at Great Lakes Naval Training Center.

Meanwhile, I was about to go on the most exciting part of my stint in the Navy. In January 1947, we got orders for a special goodwill assignment and nobody knew where we were going. We went to sea out of Philadelphia and the captain announced we were going up the Mississippi to New Orleans and to be the receiving ship for Mardi gras in February. I said to myself here I am, making up for what I missed at home during the

V-J Day Celebration in downtown Portsmouth. The captain said there had never been a Navy ship this size that far up the Mississippi to New Orleans. The maneuvering was unbelievable. We had to make hairpin turns, then had to back down, then two-thirds forward and flank speed, and back. I was on the boiler front being trained as a boiler tender.

So we had two weeks to "turn-too" at sea, and get the ship ready. Everybody had to clean their duty station and make preparations for entering port.

When we came up the Mississippi we had bunting and flags going from the bow to the stern and up the main mast and down. It was quite a showpiece. People gathered at dockside, we tied up right at the end of Canal Street, which is the main thoroughfare of New Orleans. We opened the ship up for tours and they came by the hundreds. Mardi gras was scheduled to start three days after we arrived. It was party time. The sailors were given liberty, and we had to be in dress whites. We didn't have to be back on board the ship until seven in the morning. They loved us.

I took in the Mardi gras, went up Bourbon Street to the French Quarter. I'll never forget one incident. An older black lady was pushed off the sidewalk. Now, this was 1947, and the racial issue was still prevalent in the south. This lady was pushed off the sidewalk and her bag of groceries was strewn about. I stooped down to pick her up to try to help her. I was trying to put the canned goods back into her two bags of groceries, and I sensed that I was being watched. I looked up and there was a crowd of people just looking down at me. Another sailor grabbed me and said, "Sailor, let's get out of here. You're not supposed to do that," and he grabbed me and we lost ourselves in the crowd. That was my first experiences of racial prejudice. My boat was integrated. We never had a problem aboard our ship.

I had my chance to go either into engineering or the deck force. But I saw guys holly stoning the decks, do you know what that is? Every Friday they'd get a rock—it looked like a brick—with a hole in the middle. A stake goes into the hole and a bosun's mate with a water hose would start to "holly stone" the wooden decks. They'd go back and forth with a stone on a stick, and grind each plank down so that it was white again. The bosun's mate would tell you to move up to the next plank and there were probably 200 planks that would go across the deck. You'd get all the bubble gum and grease and the tobacco juice. I said to myself "Deck force isn't for me," so I asked for the engineering department and they put me in the boiler room as a boiler tender/striker. I kind of liked the work.

I was being taught how to stand watches in the boiler room and keep a working steam pressure going back to the engine rooms, which was obviously the propulsion unit, and so it was an important position. I made third class petty officer in a very short period of time.

At sea we were mostly standing our watches. We'd stand four to eight, and I'd go to the boiler room, watch gauges, and make sure the pressure was up and I'd be there for four hours. I did that until eight o'clock in the morning—then I was off again until four o'clock in the afternoon. The next week my watch might be shifted. Marine and stationary engineering were trades I was interesting in following when I got out of the Navy.

When we were underway we really had no recreation. We had a recreation room and we could take our eight hours off there, or we could catch up on our sleep, or letter writing—most of the time we were doing your laundry, and studying.

In the mess hall we ate in certain divisions. For instance, all the engineering division ate at once. The food was good—better than eating at home. Homemade pies—they had a bakery aboard. We also had a cobbler shop, a barbershop, and a small laundry. This was a heavy cruiser, the next size down from a battleship. We were usually out to sea four to five weeks before coming back to port. We'd come back in Friday and then have leave until Monday morning. We were picking up supplies, drilling with general quarters, and firing the eight-inch gun at targets in the distance. We were still preparing to defend our country.

I loved being at sea. I loved being topside—the sunrises, the sunsets. No matter what watch I stood I always tried to be up at sunrise in the Caribbean. It was beautiful, beautiful, beautiful. The water was so blue and pretty. This was all new to me. I had never been further from home than Hampton Beach and so I made the most of it.

Around the latter part of August in 1947, I got my orders to be transferred. The Navy needed some boiler tenders on the USS *Missouri*, BB-63, which was being overhauled at the Brooklyn Naval Shipyard. I didn't like that too much, but when you get orders, you're forced to go. They needed about four boiler tenders so four of us off the *Macon* were transferred to the USS *Missouri*. They were tearing down the boilers, and renewing all the valves and gauges. The *Missouri* had seen a lot of action in the war.

I got my orders when we were in port from the yeoman's office at

Philadelphia Naval Shipyard. Usually when you're transferred to another ship you're given some orders that allow you two or three days at home. I had to pack my sea bag and make sure it was shipped to the Brooklyn Naval Shipyard and put aboard the *Missouri*.

When I went home, I told my mother I was going to another ship and what my assignment would be. We were not getting paid much—we received an envelope with money in it on the first and 15th of every month. We'd line up in the mess hall and the paymaster from our division would have an envelope with your name on it. He'd have a big box of them and we'd get $32, $34 every pay period—all depending on how much we wanted taken out. I was having $15 a month taken out to send home to take care of the family and pay my board as I always did. It was a habit and my mother appreciated it. I could go for long periods at sea where I didn't really need any money.

So I was transferred to the USS *Missouri*, which was in dry dock. I took the bus down from Boston to Brooklyn. The Navy was almost ready to put the ship together.

1947—U.S.S. *Missouri* (BB 63)

I couldn't believe that I had been assigned to this battleship that had been instrumental in the surrender of the Japanese. The ceremony, held on Sept. 2, 1945, as the ship was anchored in Tokyo Bay, Japan, ended World War II. My first interest was to view the plate in the deck where Gen. Douglas MacArthur and the foreign dignitaries stood for this historical event. There were four battle ships in the fleet during that time. All classed as the same size, they were USS *Wisconsin*, USS *Iowa*, USS *New Jersey*, and the *Missouri*.

My second interest was in viewing this massive battleship from the bottom of the dry dock. The hull and kneel were so huge that I wondered how a ship this size could stay afloat. The ship was in much need of repair and it was to take at least six months before it would be ready for sea.

I was assigned to one of the four boiler rooms. Each of these "fire rooms" had two boilers "back to back," which were capable of delivering steam to the engine room that would produce speeds of up 43 knots— which was very fast at that these time.

The main purpose of the battleships was to carry the 16-inch guns, which could fire at a target fifteen miles off shore. This was 1948 when

Two views of the USS Missouri. (Above) The Japanese government signed surrender documents aboard the Missouri *on September 2, 1945. (Below) The* Missouri *firing her sixteen-inch guns.*

The USS Missouri in drydock.

there was no satellite tracking, and we only had radar and observers who could say where to fire the guns.

I reported to my engineering division officer and was assigned to one of the fire rooms. I was in "B" Division and got my bunk. It was four bunks high on this ship; on the other it had been three. A lot of men were aboard—there were 2,200 sailors when we left Brooklyn Naval Shipyard, with a detachment of marines. At sea, we had to stand at attention in dress blues each morning, and present ourselves to the colors and then go down and change into our dungarees and work shirts for working. The Marines would present the colors at eight o'clock and they had a band aboard the battleship that would play—very regulation—although we had a different name for it.

As a sailor we had our whites, blues and, dungarees. The dress whites were for any time we were in a climate, such as the tropics, where whites should be worn. Dress blues are for a colder climate.

When we left the ship, we were inspected to make sure our shoes were shined, cuffs were down, neckerchiefs were in a V on the jumpers and our hats were squared away. Very, very strict on dress—in fact, at two o'clock in the morning I got caught in North Station in Boston at a counter having a cup of coffee with my hat on the back of my head and my jumper cuffs turned up. The shore patrol came over and wrote me up as out of uniform.

The ship needed a six-month complete overhaul at the Brooklyn Navy Yard. We did a complete rip-out of the boiler room and engineering areas. We took out all the lagging—the covering—from the steam lines and the valves. We put new lagging on, and that's where I picked up a little asbestos lung damage. We rebuilt many of the valves, the gauges, and pumps—mostly pumps—and flushed the boilers and cleaned the tubes. It was tough work—it was really a lot of bull work.

We'd sleep in our compartments when we were doing this work, stayed right aboard the ship, and ate aboard the ship. Mostly the work was done on the engineering deck, which is the third deck down. The first deck was the mess deck, where all the administrative officers were and where we ate. The second deck was berthing, and the third deck was engineering, the engine room, the boiler room, and all the auxiliaries' spaces. It was pretty tight conditions. When we left port from Brooklyn Naval Shipyard after overhaul, with 2,200 men aboard—it was like a floating city, but there would be fewer men aboard then than in wartime.

New York, New York

I went into Times Square every night with a group of four or five; we never went into town alone. We came back that way, too, in a cab, all the way from Manhattan to Brooklyn Naval Shipyard—they'd let us off at the front gate. The ship was docked in a tough section of Brooklyn.

It was interesting, the first time in New York City, with all the entertainment and the clubs. The uniformed, military person was catered to—we got special rates at all the movies and shows. There were special rates in the windows of certain restaurants: ten percent discount for servicemen in uniform. Even though the war was over, people knew how important the servicemen were.

We went to the old Cotton Club. I had often heard about it and I wanted to go there because I liked jazz. Everyone was dressed up, as it was an elite place, everyone in tuxes, and long gowns for the women. Servicemen were welcomed at the bar. I enjoyed just walking through Central Park and being in Times Square—the excitement, the nightlife, the traffic, the lights. I enjoyed riding the subway, too. If you were in uniform there was always a New Yorker to assist, "Sailor, can I help you?"

The Brooklyn Navy Yard was booming. They were doing a lot of overhauls and repairs to our naval ships that had been at sea for a long time during the war. The yard workers were dedicated.

After the overhaul we went to sea, fired the sixteen-inch guns, and had training aboard ship. We were called to battle stations every once in a while and had man overboard drills. We had training for fire drills, and

Harold in dress whites at San Juan. Puerto Rico.

keeping the ship ship-shape, even though the war was over.

The living quarters were four bunks high. I liked the top bunk even if we were cruising in the Caribbean, because it was the hottest. I always tried to keep a fan rigged up so it would blow right on me. I had a little more room on the top—the other bunks only had as much as eighteen or twenty inches between them. I didn't want the bottom one, because guys sit on it, or the middle ones because they would stand on it to get to the top, so the top bunk was always better. There were maybe seventy-five to eighty guys in a compartment.

The people in the ports of call were always friendly to American sailors. We'd be underway at sea two-to-three weeks at a time before reaching port. Tour guides would show people from the city around the ship, which was decked out with flags and bunting. If you had a band aboard—the band would play. Coming up the gangway the tourists would love it. The *Missouri* was huge, but people weren't allowed in the secure places, like down below in the engine room or the fire room. They mostly stayed topside and around the gun turrets and around the bridge area. The first thing people wanted to see, around the bow, was the place where the signing of the 1945 peace treaty took place on Sept. 2nd.

At holidays we divided the crew in half: we either went home at Thanksgiving or at Christmas. I chose to go home at Christmas. Thanksgiving aboard the *Missouri* was very elegant. I still have the menu from 1947—from soup to nuts, a gourmet meal, roast turkey, hams, chicken, the whole bit. We had our choice—we couldn't ask for a better meal.

Christmas was routine in 1947. I spent my ten-day leave at home in our new house. I brought each one of my brothers and sisters a little gift from New York City, all wrapped up. I spent New Year's in Times Square in 1947 into 1948—it was like one big party. It was very exciting.

We went out to sea in January or February, and then I was discharged. I had made third class and the Navy wanted to give me second-class if I signed over for four more years. I said no. They said I had sixty days to sign after my discharge and I could come back in the Navy with the same rate and the same privileges. I decided to go home and see what there was for jobs and I wanted to go to school. I was going to use the GI Bill.

Everybody had heard of the *Missouri* and they wanted to see it. So I sent home pictures and all kinds of mementos and things we had aboard.

When we enlisted we were given a date when our discharge date was going to be. I actually got out two months early because I had signed up for the stand-by reserves—I regretted when the Korean War started. I didn't remember signing up for what they called ready reserves. That means I was on stand-by, but not required to go to any meetings or any drills. My name was just on a list and if the military needed to call up any reservists I'd be one of the first ones. So when the Korean War started, I was called up.

But I got out of the Navy in April 1948. I was shipped to Norfolk, Virginia, where I joined several hundred others being discharged. We went through a lot of paper work with the yeoman and turned in certain personal items the Navy requires. These were some manuals and books I had that pertained to my rate. The Navy wanted to know if I had any weapons issued me and I said no—I wasn't part of any assault team. On any large ship they divide a small group into what they call an emergency assault team, but I wasn't part of that.

It takes about a week or ten days to be completely discharged. We were given a complete physical and every day a talk as to what it's like out there in civilian life. We were told what our benefits were as a veteran under the GI Bill. I joined what they called the "52-20 Club"—$20 a week for fifty-two weeks for all veterans.

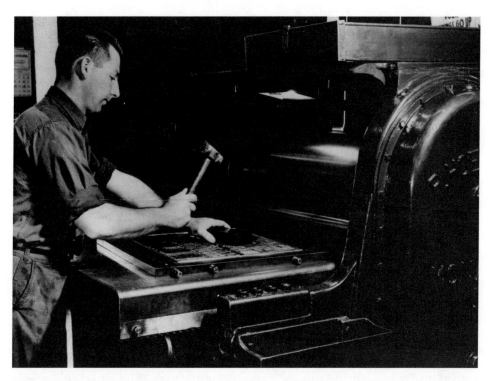

Pressman Bill planes a chase, a metal page of type and advertisements, to make ready for printing.

I was assigned to duties at the base, such as cleaning barracks—a crummy duty. I hated it. I mean, I was on my way out. If someone said he was a truck driver they'd give him a wheelbarrow. "Any truck drivers here?" the C.O. would ask, and all the truck drivers would line up and they took them behind the barracks and give them a wheelbarrow and a shovel.

So I came home and, with a lot of other discharged men, we met every morning downtown, in front of Jarvis's, just about the same as today in front of the North Church. We talked about what we were going to do, but there weren't many jobs. Some of the boys were going to go to UNH, but I knew that my high school marks weren't that good. I did apply at the Maine Maritime Academy in Castine, Maine. I wanted to go into the Merchant Marines, I loved going to sea. I sent my records in and I received a reply in about ten days that I was rejected because I didn't have the required math to get in. They said to go back to high school and take some geometry and algebra and apply again.

Harold rented a room in the house at left on Sheafe Street..

A lot of us went down to Connecticut, but I was the only one who didn't get a job at the Pratt & Whitney Plant. Jet engines were just coming into popularity—all the planes were changing over. The jet engine was a monstrous, state-of-the art kind of propulsion and the company was hiring for good jobs. Many of my friends went there in 1949 and 1950 and worked their way up to supervisory positions and they stayed there thirty-five to forty years. They had to move down there, but I didn't want to be away from the city I grew up in.

I went back to the *Herald*—that was my second choice. From the 52-20 Club I took $20 for about three weeks. At the Veteran's Affairs Office on High Street, you could sign up on a Monday morning and on a Wednesday receive a check in the mail. You could do that for 52 weeks, but once you received a job you had to notify them and would be taken off the list. I gave them my service number—5736583—I'll always remember that. So I collected for about three weeks.

That $20 took us a long way. It bought gas, meals, and it gave us a good time. We could take a girl out on a date and we had money left over. I moved back at the new home on Madison Street, but I didn't like it—I didn't stay very long. It was still—"Home by 9!" Here I was, almost twenty years old—"Home by 9!" The only time I could stay out late was when my father was on the afternoon shift. He left at 3 o'clock and came home

The DeWitt Hotel on Porter Street was torn down to make space for the Herald's *parking lot.*

at 11:30 and my mother would allow me to go to a movie or a dance, but I had to be home before my father.

So I moved out. I took a room down on Sheafe Street, almost down to the South End, but not quite. It was $7 a week, but I had all my meals at home. I had a full-time job at the *Herald*, still in the press department, and I bought a 1949 Chevy, brand new.

The state of New Hampshire gave a bonus of $75 to all veterans. I hadn't saved any money while I was in the Navy. I had sent $15 home to my mother every pay period to help around the house, but otherwise I spent every cent while I was in the Navy.

I was on my own for the first time but I didn't like it—I didn't like being alone. I used to stay at Gilley's Dog Cart until one or two o'clock in the morning just to talk to someone. But I was still going with the girl in Rochester. I loved to dance and we were going around to different places and life was pretty good. We'd go down to the Crystal Ballroom in Lawrence, the Totem Pole in Raynham, Mass., the Weirs, which had a dance hall, and the pier at Old Orchard Beach. When Hampton Beach Casino opened for the summer, it was our favorite, every Saturday night. We danced to the famous bands. And also the York Beach Casino, which burned down—it was along Short Sands, just as you come out of road from the Nubble. It was a beautiful casino, built like an old barn with a big dance floor and a raised stage. On the Fourth of July we'd dance at the Hampton Beach Casino to a name band and then from midnight to four in the morning at the York Beach Casino.

I loved life in Portsmouth. It was slow. I knew a lot of people. Working at the *Herald* was kind of a prestige-type job. As I left the shop at three in the afternoon I'd take a couple of "spoilers" and give them to my friends. They'd wait for me and say: "Got any spoilers? Got any free ones?" The spoilers were newspapers damaged in some way, but readable.

I stayed at the Sheafe Street apartment until I got my notice in December of 1950. I was called back into the Navy. I couldn't believe the notice. "Congratulations Seaman Whitehouse—Third class, boiler tender! You have been assigned to report to the Fargo Building on January 2nd, 1951, for duty for the next sixteen months as part of the active ready reserves." I had to turn that letter into my yeoman when I reported for duty. I had forgotten that I had joined the reserves.

I was interviewed at the Fargo Building in Boston and asked what kind of duty I'd like. I said I was single and that I'd like to go aboard a destroyer—that's a smaller ship—and I said I wanted to see some action this time. And do you know where I ended up? Two days later I was sent across the street to the Boston Naval Shipyard to an aircraft carrier, to help get it out of mothballs and back into the fleet. That meant bull work in the fire room and getting it ready to go to sea. There I was stationed in South Boston, just one hour from my home. Anyone would kill for that kind of duty.

My mother couldn't believe it. I was going back into the Navy because of the Korean Conflict. A lot of standby reserves were needed and they were going to meetings every month at the Shipyard in an organized unit. But me, I had forgotten all about joining the standby reserves. I didn't care. I was single. It was going to be an experience. I had to give my notice at the *Herald*. My employer, though, was obligated to take me back once I returned from active duty.

The Fargo Building had sleeping quarters, with large barracks and dormitory areas and we ate our meals there. I was back in uniform and spent something like seven days there, and then I was called up for a review and asked what kind of duty I'd like to have. "I'd like to go to San Diego. I'd like to pick up a destroyer with a squadron and I'd like to go to Korea." That was where the action was. I was still in my twenties. I teamed up with another guy from Portsmouth. I didn't know he was being called back, also, but he was married with a child and he didn't want to see any action.

A list was posted outside the yeoman's office. My friend and I ran down to the office, we could hardly wait. We found our names, and I was assigned to the USS *Kula Gulf*, CVE 108, a small escort carrier, stationed at the South Boston Naval Shipyard—across the street. We were going to take it out of mothballs. I was going to be there for at least six to eight months overhauling the boilers and the engines, and then, after a shakedown cruise, the ship was going to be ferrying planes over to Europe.

Now, my buddy, who was married and had one little child, got active duty on a "tin can," a destroyer, out of San Diego. He had a gunner's man rate and I had a boiler tender's rate and they needed me to bring the ship out of mothballs.

So I packed my sea bag and reported to the ship, which was in dry dock right across the way. That was where I spent eight months, and it was pretty good duty for a sailor. In Boston, I was at Faneuil Hall every night, downtown Boston. There was a lot of action, a lot of places to go, lots of things to see, lots of clubs. So for many weeks I never came home, even though I was only forty miles away.

I was a little bit older, a little more mature—even though I was in my twenties. I wanted to make up for what I had lost growing up as a child—I wanted to see things, and go places—I wanted to do things.

I made it a point to take walking tours of Boston and motorcade and bus tours. The first thing I did was go over to Old Ironsides in Charleston, and then I went to the Science Museum. I walked all through Scollay Square, which I thought was fascinating. The servicemen were treated to all kinds of discounts at the stores, ten percent off reduced price for men in uniform. Come in, they said. They really catered to the military. They hadn't forgotten what it was like during World War II and here we were in another war. Boston was a big military town—Coast Guard, Navy, Marines, and Army.

The *Kula Gulf* was an older carrier; it was converted during the war. I don't think it saw much action, but it was used to ferry planes—they'd fly off the carrier to an air station in Europe.

A battle group is made up of carriers, battleships, and is aided by destroyers and cruisers around the battle group. Also submarines and tankers, and several auxiliary ships on the flank of the group, patrolling. The battleship's function is to deploy those sixteen-inch guns to where they are most effective. A cruiser has three eight-inch mounts, and is used closer in to shore. A destroyer seeks out enemy submarines with depth charges. The tankers are for refueling ships and there were also supply ships.

My job was to work with the engineers and thirteen to fourteen firemen to rehabilitate the engineering spaces and the boiler room, and punching tubes, redoing firebrick, and renewing lagging from the steam lines. The lagging had a lot of asbestos and this was the second time I was doing this. It's a wonder I'm here today considering all the hazardous material l came in contact with.

Life at Boston Naval Shipyard was pretty good. We slept aboard the ship, which was in dry-dock, and there was liberty every other night for us—not bad at all—liberty at four p.m. and back by 7:30. We had every other long weekend, off on Friday at four and didn't have to be back until Monday morning. It was pretty good duty. Downtown Boston was within walking distance.

I found special restaurants where I loved to eat and hang out, the honky tonks and tattoo parlors at Scollay Square, all the shows—I never did get a tattoo.

I was enjoying the Navy pretty well. I got a rate and was trying to make second-class to get a little seniority. I went home maybe once a month for a weekend. I gave up my room on Sheafe Street, but when I was home I still had to be in by nine. I'm going with this girl from Rochester more seriously now. We'd go to dances, and amusement parks, and visit friends.

The ship was headed to the Caribbean for a shakedown cruise after about seven months in Boston. It was a little bit quieter on the home front than it had been during World War II. We all figured the Korea Conflict would be over in a matter of months, and it wasn't.

Many of the sailors would keep a locker room in the city and change from their uniform, but I didn't. A lot of them didn't want to bother with the shore patrol, so they shifted into civvies, as they say.

Every day I had to go to my work station, the number one boiler room, aboard the *Kula Gulf*. I was working with five or six firemen in the same fire room. I got paid $35 to $40 every payday, which was the 1st and 15th of every month. All the reservists were probably a little mad that they got called back. We were in the fire room—the boiler room—and steaming out of Boston harbor when we heard from the captain, "Number one, number two fire room -you're steaming black smoke!" We looked up the periscope, which was a sight glass in each boiler room, and all we saw was black smoke, coming out of our stack. Even today I think much of the black skyline around Boston was caused by our not having the right mixture of air and oil. That black smoke rolled out of our stack, crossed the sky, and it was terrible. The captain on the bridge tried hard to find out what caused it. The boilers were being fired for the first time and not being set properly caused the smoke.

This was in September or October of 1951. We were testing our weapons and radar—testing everything. We cruised, we did full speed, we did flank speed, we backed down, and we did maneuvering to test the engines, and the rudders, to make sure everything was working.

When we got back, we got word we were going to take some planes to the Mediterranean and they'd fly off to a base over there. We weren't told what base.

So we pulled into Charleston, South Carolina, to take on planes. They didn't fly on but were hoisted aboard from dockside. We headed across the Atlantic, with probably fifteen to twenty prop planes. We took on the airdales—that's what they were called—the crew that handled all planes. They were the mechanics, flight engineers, and the flight deck crew. They took care of the landings and the taking off, the upkeep —and the pilots, as well.

We were in Charleston maybe four, five days, and then left for sea. The ship had flight quarters where pilots practiced landing and taking off. I used to sneak on to the fantail—everybody's supposed to be secured to their battle stations, you're not supposed to go topside—but I went up to the stern and watched as the planes came right over me. I'd peek my head around to the catwalk and see the arresting gear, which was the hook under the fuselage of the plane that grabbed the cable across the main deck and stopped the plane. If the pilot missed that cable he goes into a netted barrier, but that could wreck the plane. The prop would go right into it. But I never saw a time when a plane missed the hook. Those pilots were good. We had flight quarters four or five times going across the Atlantic. They trained for night flights and early morning flights.

When we got to the Mediterranean the planes took off to wherever they were going and we pulled into Gibraltar. I'd never been to Europe before. I felt I could reach out and touch the Rock of Gibraltar; it was so close as we're went through the Straights.

We anchored and took our motor launches into Gibraltar. I took a bus tour with a couple friends and we went to the outskirts and went to the top of the mountain, and overlooked from one entrance of the Mediterranean to the other. It was interesting, seeing how the people were living. We had some good times during the short time we were there. We left Gibraltar, still maneuvering, as we came home—no flight quarters, of course—but the airdales were still aboard. We got to Charleston and all the airdales got off—it was a fairly quick trip.

By April of 1952 was happy to get out of the Navy again. I was discharged and headed back to Portsmouth. I was twenty-one-years old, and a veteran of two wars. I didn't know exactly what I was going to do, but I got thinking about the *Herald* again. My friend Bill Coldwell, who was production manager in the press department, says to me, "You got your GI Bill?" I said, "Yeah." And he said, "'Why don't you take an apprenticeship in the composing room as a printer?" So he lined up a meeting with the publisher. I told him I had my GI Bill, and they had another meeting with a representative who came down from the Department of Education in Concord, and we set up a schedule of what my four-year apprenticeship would entail. I'd have six months of this kind of work, and after six months more I'd move up. There was a specialist's segment of learning and training that I would get and I was making a journeyman's wage, which was about $100 a week. An apprentice journeyman was paid about $50, but the state was reimbursing me another $50 so I was making real journeyman's wages. I received a nice check at the end of every month and that check paid for a brand new car.

My first phase at the newspaper was for six months as a copyboy in the composing room. All I did was cut up copy coming off the Teletype and hand it to the Linotype operator who set the type.

I didn't want to leave Portsmouth. I had made up my mind. I had seen everything, done everything, and been everywhere—even though I hadn't really been everywhere. But I wanted to be in Portsmouth, it was my home and I said I'd never leave.

My brother was in the Navy at this point—he'd quit high school in his junior year. He was aboard another carrier, the *Valley Forge*. He was over in Korea, but I don't know if he saw much action. My father was still at the Navy Yard and mother was still working hard taking care of the new home on Madison Street.

I got another room on Sheafe Street, in the same building as the one before. It was a nice place, only $5 a week. But the bathroom was still down the hallway and I wanted my own bathroom. I was getting kind of lonesome because all my friends were getting married. We were all in our mid-twenties, and they were getting married. They had graduated from college and moved from the city to big corporations and firms. Things were changing socially.

Chapter Five: Working at the
Portsmouth Herald

1952

My apprenticeship at the *Herald* had a highly skilled technical title to the job. After four years of apprenticeship training, I would have the title of "compositor—Linotype operator" or newspaper printer. The newspaper business was very exciting during this era, the most important news media other than radio and movie newsreels.

The mechanical department at the Herald was considered "family." That is, basically all the same age group—raising our families, sharing our problems, and helping one another in building our dream homes—pouring a cement floor, or the following week shielding a new roof.

Whenever a new baby came into the family we took a five-minute break from the workday to cerebrate. The cigars and candy would be passed out. Even though some of us did not smoke, we lit up for the special occasion. The cigar smoke was so thick, as the old saying goes, we could cut it with a knife.

We called each other by nicknames, such as, "Cass," "Goodie," "Rip," "Tose," "Rooly," and "Spin." Of course I was known as "Whitey," a name taken from my father. I'll never forget "Horse," "Big lou," and "Peanut." And then there was the "Kid," still referred today to as "the Story Teller." Even the supervisors were called by their nicknames, such as, "AC," "WC," and "JD."

So being employed for the only newspaper in town had a certain cache to it. The pay was minimal, but there was job security and the closeness of "family relationship" made it very rewarding. Each day that I left work at 3:00 p.m. I would take three or four *Herald* spoilers with me to pass out to my friends. It was routine to have coffee at Jarvis' Restaurant after each workday. I would be asked many times, "Whitey, what's new?" Anyone who worked for a newspaper was considered to have the latest

Harold and Ruthie on a date in 1953.

news. Publisher J.D. Hartford sponsored a Christmas party for all employees and their families. This was held at the Rockingham Ballroom on State
Street, and would include a meal, gifts, and a picture of the employee's
children—a time that we all looked forward to.

1953-54

Portsmouth was becoming a city where you could not make a living and
raise a family. In the central business district there were boarded up storefronts. People who went off to college after high school never returned,

(above) The Herald *plate-making room. (below) Harold, left, in* Portsmouth Herald *plant on Porter Street.*

unless their family had a business that they could help with. I still had a
room in a boarding house on Sheafe Street. Found it very lonesome living
alone. Ruth and I were dating quite often now. We would travel fifty to sixty
miles on a Saturday night to ballroom dance. By the time we were in our late
twenties we had seen every dance band that was popular at that time.

1955

Early in the year Ruthie and I decided we would get married. We were
both nearly thirty years old, and it was time to settle down and have a family. Having several children was our goal.

1955-May 14

We had a church wedding with a reception at the Portsmouth Yacht Club
and we honeymooned in Florida—driving to and from in a brand-new
1955 Chevy. On returning, we settled in a rented apartment at 1195 South
Street. We referred to that location as the outskirts of the South End. The
rent was $65.00 a month with heat included. Our first child, Karen Rae
,was born, on June 26, 1959. Three years later on July 12, 1962, Brian Scott,
our son was born. At that time we did not realize that that would be the
extent of our family—so much for a large family.

1959-60

Banks that had a prospect for growing were buying the downtown property—demolishing the older buildings, rebuilding, and creating parking
lots. The federal program of urban renewal was debated by the city council and final approval was given. The government classed the northern section of the city as a blighted area, so federal funds became available. Most
of the older houses on Hanover, Vaughn, Russell, and Deer Streets were
bull dosed under. Rebuilding would have a positive effect on our economy—so said the federal government. Many of the Italian families were
forced to move, breaking up years of close relationships, which created
some serious hardships. It was a program that in later years proved not to
be in the best interest of the community, both economically and socially.
Portsmouth had the last urban renewal program of its kind.

1961

The colonial restoration project called Strawbery Banke, Inc. was incorpo-
rated, with the persistence of Miss Dorothy Vaughn, as well as some known

Harold's Strawbery Banke stock certificate.

historical preservationists. The first stockholders' meeting was held on November 15, 1961. I felt so strongly about this project at that time that I bought three shares of stock at $10.00 each. That was a large sum of money to me then. The first meeting was held at the Rockingham Ballroom on State Street. According to a stockholders' notice, there were six items to be voted upon, excluding a slate of officers and a committee recommendation of a slate of directors. It was a very exciting period for the South End. We all knew that suddenly our home value would increase. People would be buying in the South End in order to have a piece of Portsmouth's history.

1962

At the *Herald*, our publisher, J.D. Hartford, notified his employees that an option had been made with the federal government to purchase two vacant lots in the urban renewal area. The lots were located across the tracks off Raines Avenue. This would be the future home of the newspaper. We all questioned the location. "Mr. Hartford, it's too far out of downtown. No business has ever made it in that section of the city." We were very concerned.

1963

March 18—the untimely death of our publisher was a real shock to all of us at the *Herald*. Who would manage the every day publishing of the only newspaper in the city? What about the new plant? Would the paper be sold? These were major questions among us long time employees.

One day in April, an item appeared in the *Herald* stating that seven parcels of property would be put up for sale. These were lots had been taken over by the city for nonpayment of taxes. One of the lots was located on Humphrey Court directly behind the Haven School, where I had played baseball and football many times on a Saturday afternoon. One week later I received a notice from the city clerk that my bid was the highest. I was the proud owner of a piece of property in the South End—one of the happiest days of my life. My first tax bill was $13.95 for a vacant piece of land.

I had completed my apprenticeship at the *Herald* and was starting to raise a family. I noticed that the South End of Portsmouth was going through major changes—old abandoned cars, scrap metal, old stoves, and refrigerators were slowly disappearing. People were beginning to take pride in their neighborhood and their property.

Strawbery Banke

I joined Miss Dorothy Vaughn and her team of historical preservationists, usually sitting in the background while she spoke to groups about how important it was to save Portsmouth's history. She wanted to stop the destruction of this city's greatest assets—our older houses. The huge brick buildings such as the Farragut School, County Court House, and a late-1700s Baptist church on the corner of State and Middle Streets were destroyed to make way for economic development.

The Raynes Avenve- Maplewood Avenue area before urban renewal. After the houses in the center were torn down, the Hearld, *which had supported urban renewal purchased the parcel for its offices and printing plant.*

1964 Urban Renewal
The federal North End urban renewal project had displaced nearly 900-950 people. Many nationalities especially the Italians were forced to give up their homes and family-owned businesses. My aunt and uncle, who had lived all their lives in their home on Deer Street across from the railroad station, were relocated to Atlantic Heights. They lived out the rest of their lives in an area that they were not really happy with. My cousin, Donald,

who had settled in Baltimore with his family, tried to comfort his father and mother, with many visits back home. He shared relationships and memories of younger days of growing up on Deer Street as a close-knit group.

Some twenty-five acres, as well as many small businesses, were leveled for future development. One business that I remember going to, whenever my mother made a visit to see her sister, was the old Peganellie Store on the corner of Deer and Vaughn Streets. I remember always the smell of spaghetti sauce coming from the back room, saw dust on the floor, fresh bread hanging from an overhead basket, penny candy, and small portions of meat displayed in a showcase. It was a store that had not changed in the last 100 years.

After the 250 homes and some 60 businesses were bulldozed to make way for a "better Portsmouth," the land stayed vacant for many years, mainly because the developers did not trust the government when discount construction loans were offered. Soon after Portsmouth's North End urban renewal project was finished, the whole federal program was abandoned.

The landlords and homeowners in the South End realized that the same concept could take place in their neighborhood. More emphasis was then put on repairs and updating homes. So, with the development of Strawbery Banke and Prescott Park, the waterfront South End became a section of Portsmouth that people saw as a small part of the city's history—a complete turn-around in a once poor neighborhood.

1967

This was the year my family and I made plans for a new Humphrey Court home. It would be a three-bedroom raised ranch with a fireplace and a cellar garage. Because of the amount of ledge on the lot, we knew we wouldn't be able to get a full cellar and getting water and sewage lines to the house was questionable. As the bulldozer started to clear the lot, it was apparent that there was not as much ledge as expected. My bank construction loan was approved at that time, and allowed us to get the shell of the house built. Once the roof windows and siding were in place, I took over.

In order to purchase building supplies weekly, I took a part-time job at a gas station working three nights a week, around the corner from the *Herald*—which made it quite convenient. I was glad to get this part-time job because I was getting 75 cents an hour, not a bad hourly wage at

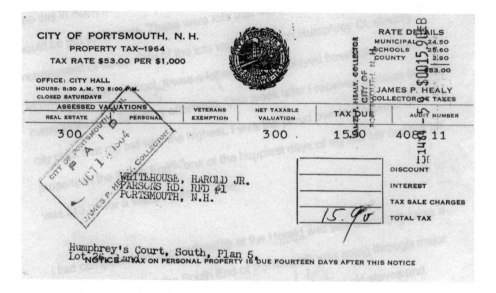

The original tax bill for 58 Humphrey's Court.

The Whitehouse home at 58 Humphrey's Court.

that time, just for pumping gas and changing oil. I made many new friends because the boss said that I could give a two-cent discount per gallon to the good customers—they all seem to be good customers.

1968

After working on the house nights and weekends, we moved in. It was a proud family event because I was living in a house on a lot where I played football and baseball. Our house was far from being completed, but we could finish it on our own time. Its colonial design seemed to blend in with the old South End. The windows, doors, and siding had the same look as the other houses on the street. My fireplace was built from old "water struck" bricks, that were saved from the 1790 Baptist church on the corner of State and Middle Streets that was demolished in the late 1950's to make way for a gas station.

1969

This year my two children left the Haven School to enter the new Little Harbor School that was built in the Brackett Field area, along the banks of the back channel. I transferred my PTA interest and special events involvement along into the new school.

1970

At this time, the "Open Concept" design of the Little Harbor School was being questioned. Many parents and older teachers noticed that this new "state of the art" teaching was not working. Slowly the system changed to the old standard of individual rooms, but only after many hours of debate and study, was that was allowed. The "Open Concept" way of teaching was never mentioned again.

1971

After the death of the *Herald's* publisher in March of 1963, the department heads had been left the controlling shares in his will. Later, the seven stockholders sold the paper to an English firm known as the Thompson Corp.

Late 1971 Herald Breaks Ground

The new plant at 11 Maplewood Avenue was to be a state of the art building with room for future expansion. A brick-faced and steel framed structure, it was air conditioned, with loading ramps on both ends. The openness of the newsroom was a new design. But we employees were still skeptical about locating out of downtown area, across the tracks. It was one of the first developments within the urban renewal area.

1972 Moving Day at the Herald

The plan was, that after the press run on the Friday afternoon, we employees in the "back shop" would help the moving company in relocating the heavy equipment—metal cutting saws, routers, planners, the plate finishing machine, and five Linotypes. The printers and pressman were excited for the opportunity to receive over-time pay for Saturday and Sunday—knowing that we would be working far in the night hours.

I chose not to volunteer for this weekend work, but instead I wanted to record this historical event on 8 mm movie film with my Brownie camera. This was a hobby that I had started about ten years earlier when my two children were born. There was only one drawback to this hobby: the four 150-watt bulb bar lights that had to be on for clear recording. All my friends resented this hobby of mine. Even then, the finished movies were very poor, black and white, with fading light and subjects not clear. Came Monday morning and the move was completed. Printers and pressman were excited to be in their new home, the paper was "put to bed" at 2:00 p.m. and presses were rolling for the afternoon edition.

1974 Caught up in a R.I.F.

A new person was shown through the plant at the *Herald* during the summer of 1974. He appeared to just be looking around at the production side of the newspaper—just interested in the way the newspaper was operating. We were told that he was a production manager from another newspaper that the company owned. He was there to gain information on cost savings and report parent company. But, with his everyday appearance, we became more and more skeptical. Our wondering proved to be what we as a "printer's family" dreaded to hear—by the end of the summer, there would be a reduction in force—eight-long time employees would be terminated. With only three days to settle with the payroll department for leave and insurance and severance pay, it was a shocker to all of us. We all had worked together for twenty to twenty-five years.

The eight employees' reduction list, which included my name, was announced on a Wednesday, and Friday was be our last day. After twenty-eight years as a printer and part time pressman, I would be looking for work. At the age of forty-eight, this was new for me and I had to put together a resume that had only one employer and one trade I knew. So every day I would head off in the early morning, contacting every printer that I knew personally. The economy at that time was very weak and employment was down.

1974—1976

The printing trade had changed drastically. Photocomposition had replaced the old "hot lead," raised-type method of printing. It was difficult to adjust. So, after working on a part time basis at UNH and other print shops, I knew that my trade was no longer a highly skilled profession. A change in job skills was necessary. I went to work at the Portsmouth Naval Shipyard and remained there for more than twenty years.

Friendly rivals South Ender Harold Whitehouse and Puddle Docker George F. wearing their 1940 jackets at the 1982 Puddle dock reunion attended by over 500 people at Yoken's Restaurant.

PUDDLE DOCK REUNION

"A Reunion for all Puddle Dockers and Friends"
(only 500 tickets available)

Saturday, May 29, 1982   6:00 to 10:00 p.m.

at

Yoken's Restaurant

HAPPY HOUR   6:00 p.m. to 7:00 p.m.

Buffet Style Dinner
served at 7:00 p.m.
Tickets Required
(No tickets available at the door.)

Music by Jim McMullen

Admission: $12.50
Tickets can be obtained by writing:
Puddle Dock Reunion
P.O. Box 4249, Portsmouth, N.H.
or Call 436-1491
or

George's Auto Body   *Portsmouth Public Library*

Leslie's Flower Shop

"The Puddle Dock Reunion Committee"

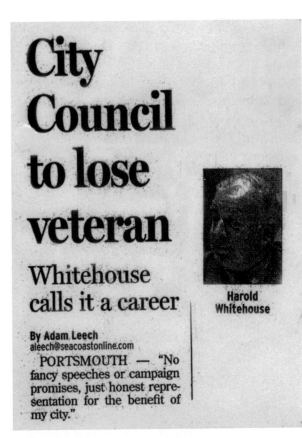

City **Council** **to lose** **veteran**

Whitehouse calls it a career

Harold
Whitehouse

By Adam Leech
aleech@seacoastonline.com

PORTSMOUTH — "No fancy speeches or campaign promises, just honest representation for the benefit of my city."

City Council Meeting, August 20, 2007

It had been a long meeting with many important agenda items. So, under the heading of miscellaneous and unfinished business, as a councilor I brought up a brief item that surprised everyone: "My fellow councilors and viewing public, I will not be seeking reelection come this November 6, 2007." Thus ended my thirty-one-year career as an elected public servant for the city of Portsmouth, New Hampshire.

My career started in 1973 as an elected school board member, mainly because of my two children in the public school system. As the years progressed, my name appeared on the ballot twelve times and I was elected each time. I served sixteen years on the school board, one year on the charter revision committee, two years a police commissioner, and twelve years as a city councilor (although at times over the years I would take a year or so rest from public office).

Someone mentioned that this could have been a record-setting event. But my only concern was, did I make a difference along the way? I think I did.

Reporters have asked me what elected position as a part of a team did I feel accomplished the most. Without any hesitation: "My sixteen years on the school board." Even today, as during those early years, contracts, curriculum, budgeting, teacher qualifications, and course offerings are important.

After being elected to the city council, I found that doing more than just reading the minutes of various meetings was not informative. So, over the years I was known to attend most public meetings, significant or not. Usually sitting quietly in the back row, I'd take notes on information, which helped me in my decision-making later. The mayor said, after my announcement, that Councilor Whitehouse was probably the hardest working elected official he had ever seen. My knowledge of the historic South End had been extremely helpful to the entire council. I would chime in on any conversation with a historic perspective, which so few people in local government knew.

My announcement at an early stage was with the hope of attracting younger candidates. It certainly is a young person's game, which requires the energy to attend many long meetings.

My last statement was that I was healthy and hoped to stay that way. Now I will be able to spend more time watching my two junior high school-aged grandchildren, Kylie and Alyxandra, participate in sporting events.

Thank you to the city of Portsmouth, New Hampshire. It has been a pleasure.

"Whitey"

From a *Portsmouth Herald* editorial, December 28, 2007, entitled

"Thank you, departing officials for your work."

Harold Whitehouse, with 12 years on the City Council, 16 years on the School Board, and two years as a police commissioner, a total of 30 years of dedicated service to the people of Portsmouth. Harold was always looking out for the people of the South End and the Puddle Dock area. His dedication and hard work as a member of the Peirce Island Committee has ensured that it will always be a recreation area. Harold always portrayed himself as a voice of "the working class," and he did it well. He was always well prepared and asked the right questions. All of the celebrations in the city that serve refreshments will certainly miss Councilor Whitehouse, as he always made time to be there if food was being served.

Epilogue 2008: Fast Track Forward

Years slip by—age has crept up. I cannot believe that I have turned around twice and I am near eighty years old. My mother and father have passed away and out of six children, just three are left—my two sisters, June and Audrey, and I. My family is now my wife, children Brian and Karen and grandchildren Kylie and Alyxandra.

There have been many articles written about the old South End, but to live through some of the events is an experience of undocumented history. Many of my childhood experiences will never be shared by the next generation. There is history and character in the old South End. I worry that if there isn't some strict control, it could be all destroyed. Trying to retain the old image of this neighborhood has been difficult. This section of the city is all that is left of the original Portsmouth.

Because of the "spotlight" in certain magazines such as *Money, Cosmopolitan, UTNE Reader,* and several retirement publications, Portsmouth is considered one of the most desirable place to live. People have found us—particularly in the South End. When the "City of the Open Door" is mentioned, the South End is described as being only a fifteen-minute walk to any place in Portsmouth.

An important natural resource is the waterfront and its view. It provides and enhances the beauty—this is what attracts so many people. Housing costs have increased drastically because of this element. The late-1800 houses are in demand because people want a part of Portsmouth's history.

However, as I view some areas along the waterfront, I have noticed that the city has ignored this old section and its architectural heritage, and allowed developers to demolish some homes. The rebuilding has been extremely out of proportion, thus completely changing the character of the neighborhood. But the trade-off is additional tax money to the city, so say the developers. As I walk down the side streets and along the waterfront, the changes I see are enormous. Where once stood a variety of home styles—colonials, capes and New Englanders—new additions and

Grandchildren Kylie and Alyxandra, Harold and Ruth's pride and joy.

encroachment have been allowed. Every bit of "green space" and available land has been lost with additions to older homes.

No longer are there abandoned car parts, stoves, and refrigerators left in vacant lots, but the beautiful, rich soil of back yards that once grew healthy vegetables has been plowed under—especially if there is a view of any part of the river. Many of the narrow streets and sidewalks have been revamped with granite curbing, brick, and plantings. Engineers have designed the streetscape with what they call "bump outs"—a form of traffic control.

People who came to Portsmouth during the last twenty years, chose this section of the city because its on the fringe of Prescott Park and Strawbery Banke and also because of their fondness for a part of Portsmouth's history. They realize what a special quality of life is like living in view of the old waterfront. But this has created a very expensive atmosphere for survivors to live in. Many of my long-time friends have moved away, selling their homes, because of the taxes, insurance, and cost of upkeep.

(above) Historic Baptist church, at the corner of State and Middle Streets, was torn down to make way for a gas station. (below) Rockingham Country Courthouse on State Street, played host to the Japanese and Russian delegates who negotiated the treaty of Portsmouth in 1905, but it was torn down in the 1960s to make way for a bank parking lot.

I am still here for now—living at 58 Humphrey Court—a short street connecting Marcy Street and Newcastle Avenue. This has been my home for over forty years, a move from my childhood days of a distance of about hundred feet, from 76 South School Street. Ruth and I have been living in this house since we built it.

I am still telling stories to the newcomers of what it was like back "you know when." My stories have been the topic of many conversations about the real South End. Brian and Karen often ask me to explain again the closeness of family life while growing up here, how we went without. But as my mother would always say, "We were not poor. We just didn't have the fancy things."

A part of growing old gracefully and enjoying it, is having these boyhood memories. I can find laughter and the sense of good fortune to have lived and remembered that era, the old South End. As an old newspaper printer would say it's a "30."